*National Security through a Cockeyed Lens*

# National Security through a Cockeyed Lens

How Cognitive Bias Impacts U.S. Foreign Policy

STEVE A. YETIV

Johns Hopkins University Press

*Baltimore*

© 2013 Johns Hopkins University Press
All rights reserved. Published 2013
Printed in the United States of America on acid-free paper
2  4  6  8  9  7  5  3  1

Johns Hopkins University Press
2715 North Charles Street
Baltimore, Maryland 21218-4363
www.press.jhu.edu

Library of Congress Cataloging-in-Publication Data

Yetiv, Steven A.
National security through a cockeyed lens : how cognitive bias impacts U.S.
foreign policy / Steve A. Yetiv.
pages cm.
Includes bibliographical references and index.
ISBN 978-1-4214-1125-5 (paperback)—ISBN 1-4214-1125-3 (paperback)—
ISBN 978-1-4214-1126-2 (electronic)—ISBN 1-4214-1126-1 (electronic)
1. National security—United States—Decision making.
2. International relations—Psychological aspects.   3. Decision
making—Psychological aspects.   I. Title.
UA23.Y37   2013
355'.033573—dc23
2013006069

A catalog record for this book is available from the British Library.

*Special discounts are available for bulk purchases of this book. For more information,
please contact Special Sales at 410-516-6936 or specialsales@press.jhu.edu.*

Johns Hopkins University Press uses environmentally friendly book
materials, including recycled text paper that is composed of at least 30 percent
post-consumer waste, whenever possible.

# CONTENTS

I started to write this book in 2002, after having several long discussions with a colleague about the extent to which countries make rational decisions. (Yes, I know, we must be nerds.) Over that time period, I incurred many intellectual debts. In particular, I thank Jennifer Cunningham, Lowell Feld, Mark Haas, Fran Jacobsen, Patrick James, Robert Jervis, Rose McDermott, Mark O'Reilly, Katerina Oskarsson, Jonathan Renshon, David Welch, and Liz Zanoni for their comments and inputs, as well as the anonymous reviewers for the Johns Hopkins University Press. Tulu Balkir, Scott Duryea, and Sagar Rijal, my research assistants over the past few years, were also helpful. I also thank my copyeditor, Ashleigh McKown, and my editor, Suzanne Flinchbaugh. Suzanne ably guided the manuscript after taking over from the late Henry Tom, who had shown initial interest in the work and who had successfully guided the projects of so many scholars.

*National Security through a Cockeyed Lens*

# Introduction

## When Psychology Meets Decision Making

In our lifetime we have witnessed a number of events that have revolutionized global politics. The Cold War—which defined the world for decades—ended. The Soviet Union fell under its own weight and international pressures. And revolutions swept across Europe and the Middle East, toppling dictators who had seemed to be permanent global fixtures. The United States faced nihilistic terrorists on September 11, 2011, and experienced long, American-led wars in faraway Iraq and Afghanistan. We saw a near meltdown of the American financial system, a massive European debt crisis that threatened to tear asunder the European Union, and rising concerns about transnational problems like climate change. Having not been transfixed by such massive change since the two world wars, many wondered if the United States was in serious decline and whether this might rearrange the architecture of world politics.

In this high-stakes era, it's especially critical to explore how we make decisions, both as laypeople and as leaders. Doing so may help us cope with the fundamental problems of our dynamic age and of our individual lives, as well as understand what shapes the world around us.

What mental errors or cognitive biases can undermine good decision making? Drawing on four decades of psychological, historical, and political science research on cognitive biases, this book illuminates some of the key pitfalls found in our leaders' decision-making processes and examines cognitive biases or mental errors in our perceptions of ourselves and our world. These biases include overconfidence, seeing what we expect to see, and focusing excessively on one factor to the neglect of others when making decisions. Just as we can point to examples where our judgment and decision making are reasonably accurate, it is not hard to find instances where significant biases cloud our thinking.

Focusing on foreign policy decision making,[1] I explore key events and developments in U.S. national security in the past four decades, especially those related to the Middle East. They range from U.S. energy policy to the war in Afghanistan in the 1980s that spawned al-Qaeda to the U.S.-led invasion of Iraq. The story of some of these events continues to unfold, including the ongoing saga in Iraq and Afghanistan and America's struggle with the consumption of oil, which has increased over time even as dependence on foreign oil has decreased in the last several years.

This book addresses a number of questions. Why has it taken the United States so long since the 1973–74 Arab oil embargo to make any significant progress in achieving energy security, even though virtually every American president has called for major moves in that direction, especially to decrease oil consumption and more recently to address climate change? What dynamics lead great powers to lock into power struggles that endanger their citizens, hurt their economies, and produce unpredictable results? Why did the United States invade Iraq in 2003, and why was the outcome so problematic, with thousands dead and much treasure lost? Why are al-Qaeda, its affiliates, and sympathizers so viciously anti-American?

Analyzing decisions, especially those in the areas of national security and foreign policy, can allow us to examine the minds of leaders and to assess what cognitive processes shaped their decisions. It can also help identify the role that cognitive factors play in the overall mix of decision making in ways that we could not discover by ignoring mental errors and processes.

## The Arguments of the Book

This book shows in five episodes of U.S. national security how cognitive biases were more influential in U.S. decision making and security than commonly believed or understood. By examining these episodes through the lens of cognitive biases, we add vital insight to our understanding of how decisions are made. I show how the distorted cognitive lens of al-Qaeda leaders contributed to the attacks on 9/11 and the ongoing conflict with America and the West; how overconfidence contributed to America's decision to invade Iraq in 2003; and how short-term thinking—a prominent cognitive bias—has contributed to America's inability to develop a comprehensive energy policy, making the Middle East more important to the United States and enhancing its proclivity to be involved in the region.

At a broader level, this book says something about rationality. One could make the case that we would be fortunate if decisions were made objectively by computers that identified options for dealing with a problem or situation, carefully weighed their costs and benefits, and picked or tried to pick the best option.[2] But of course this isn't reality. To what extent human beings and countries go through this process of rational thinking is one of the biggest questions that we face as citizens and sovereigns. This book argues that we tend to be quasi-rational; we often try to be rational, but we sometimes face cognitive biases in doing so. That view clashes with the dominant view among academics and citizens, certainly as it pertains to the behavior of states in world politics, where the behavior of states is presumably the result of rational thought that aims to maximize national interests by choosing the best among several competing options.[3] We usually explain states' decisions as if they went through a rational process of thought, weighing options and doing what was best for the country. We don't usually explain their decisions and actions as being influenced by cognitive biases such as seeing what they expected to see in world politics or focusing excessively on one factor in their calculations at the expense of other important considerations.[4] Yet much work in psychology has demonstrated the systematic ways in which individuals can deviate from rationality,[5] and drawing on such findings can enhance our understanding of how decisions are made.

What can we do to improve decision making? The final chapter of this book delves into this question and offers insights drawn from the foreign policy analysis and psychology literature, as well as my own work. Although cognitive biases are often resistant to what scholars of psychology call "debiasing," or the attempt to reduce or eliminate biases from decision making, I offer suggestions that could help U.S. decision makers and laypeople improve their decision-making processes.

## Cognitive Biases in Decision Making

Research on human cognitive fallibility, pioneered decades ago by the late Amos Tversky and Daniel Kahneman, represents the seminal achievement of modern psychological science and one key driver of the study of decision making since the 1970s. It also earned Kahneman the Nobel Prize in 2002.[6] Many political scientists, economists, and other social scientists, as well as your average layperson, assume that most human beings are rational. Kahneman and Tversky demonstrated in experiments that rationality is sometimes elusive; that mental shortcuts may contribute to bad decisions; and that decision making, while often reasonably accurate, is also frequently clouded by biases.[7]

Following in these pioneering footsteps, analysts have identified a range of errors (psychologists call them biases) in the ways that humans judge situations and evaluate risks. These biases have been documented in both real-world and laboratory settings. Some of these biases are cognitive. As explained above, this book focuses on these particular types of mental errors.[8]

Cognitive approaches often assume that decision makers are overtaxed, subject to onerous information-processing demands, faced with unreliable information and uncertainty, and under time pressure. As a result, rather than weighing costs and benefits of different options, they may consciously or subconsciously use mental shortcuts for quick, easy decisions in which they feel confident.[9] They seek to simplify reality and to make it more manageable in their own minds. Some cognitive biases may even be part of rational behavior. Using analogies as shortcuts to decision making can help illuminate how the past often informs present analysis of various options. Since people and especially policy makers are busy, shortcuts are useful and even vital in making decisions. But cognitive approaches posit centrally that individuals—and, by implication, other types of actors—are sometimes irrational or partly rational. In fact, cognitive bias is a systematic deviation from what we consider rational thinking and as such is viewed by cognitive scholars as a predictable error caused by memory, social attribution, and statistical errors.

Cognitive biases might enable faster decisions, but they can also contribute to errors in judgment and limit our capacity to find rational solutions.[10] Cognitive biases don't suggest that all decisions will be biased, but that such biases play an important role and a systematic one under certain conditions. This book demonstrates how failure to account for them can leave us with serious blind spots about decision making and its impact. As Robert Jervis has shown, U.S. Secretary of Defense John Foster Dulles routinely gave less weight to information that contradicted his prior beliefs about the Soviet Union.[11] Meanwhile, from his conspiratorial mindset, Iraqi dictator Saddam Hussein believed that the United States would invade Iraq even if he withdrew from Kuwait in the 1990–91 Persian Gulf crisis—a political impossibility from the standpoint of President George H. W. Bush, who, unlike his son, guessed correctly that Iraq would be a quagmire if America decided to invade.

Such thinking had serious costs for both Dulles and Saddam. It pushed Dulles to overemphasize the Soviet threat, possibly prolonging the Cold War. And it made Saddam less likely to understand that war with the U.S.-led coalition could be avoided,[12] making invasion more likely. The Gulf War would place Iraq at odds with the world community, shatter its economy, and contribute to yet another conflict in 2003, with massive consequences for many years thereafter.

## What This Book Contributes

Cognitive biases have been studied most generally in laboratory settings but less so in actual cases of foreign and energy policy making. We lack applications of cognitive biases for understanding American energy security, for example, even though the notions of short-term and status quo thinking are common. And while there is excellent research on overconfidence, there is less work on overconfidence as applied to international relations or to the Iraq War. Political scientist Dominic Johnson covers the Iraq War in his book *Overconfidence and War*, but not in much detail, partly because it went to print shortly after the 2003 invasion. Nor has the cognitive literature been extended in a serious way to help understand terrorism, despite the myriad arguments for why it occurs. In general, we have either excellent but brief examples of several examples of cognitive biases,[13] or in-depth analyses of one case,[14] but very little work on multiple biases in multiple foreign policy cases.

I also seek to explain what caused these biases, an effort generally undertaken in the psychology field but less commonly examined by foreign policy analysts. In the Iraq War case, I argue that overconfidence occurred because of a mix of factors: information problems, a weaker-than-usual role of the national media, post–Cold War American global dominance, misplaced analogies, and President George W. Bush's disposition and decision-making style. And in the case of al-Qaeda, this book highlights the distorted religious and political prism through which al-Qaeda and millions of its followers have seen the world, a prism that predisposes them to see what they expect to see—a central cognitive bias.

In pursuing these goals, this work may help in improving decision making. Despite the critical importance of decision making, remarkably little thought has gone into how we can improve it. As psychology professors Katherine Milkman, Dolly Chugh, and Max Bazerman argue, "the optimal moment to address the question of how to improve human decision making has arrived. Thanks to fifty years of research, psychologists have developed a detailed picture of the ways in which human judgment is bounded."[15] This book illuminates cognitive biases to help leaders and laymen avoid bad decisions and produce better ones. It may be that the role of cognitive biases is underappreciated because experimental evidence from psychology remains set apart from the study of foreign policy—not to mention American foreign policy—despite excellent work in this area.[16]

More broadly, I shed light on how the United States got involved in the Middle East over the past forty years. Cognitive biases have been largely ignored in this story, but they help explain a stream of events that are important to this tale, because they affected key decisions and, in turn, events that shaped the contours of the American regional experience.

I should stress that this book is written for a broad audience.[17] It may well be of interest to academics, but it is designed to appeal to students and educated general readers, as well.

## Foreign Policy Cases

This book examines five episodes in which cognitive biases present in the foreign policy decision-making processes of statesmen and nonstate actors may have influenced outcomes. The first focuses on the Soviet occupation of Afghanistan in the 1980s, which spawned the al-Qaeda terrorist group and the post–9/11 War in Afghanistan. The second episode is the Iran-Contra affair of the 1980s, and the third examines the origin and evolution of radical terrorism, including al-Qaeda's distorted worldview. Fourth, we examine U.S. decision making in the Iraq War of 2003. The final case is about U.S. energy policy.

I chose the episodes in the book for several reasons. They are limited to cognitive biases for which we have the most evidence, based on decades of research in psychology, history, and political science. They also involve typical biases in foreign policy and in our daily decisions, which can actually be studied via foreign policy analysis. It is not possible to examine all biases, as some are difficult to discern in the practice of foreign policy, due to either a lack of evidence or their complex and abstract nature. The framing effect is an example of cognitive bias in which one draws different conclusions from the same information, based on how that information is presented. Much evidence supports the role that this bias can play in decision making. Given the lack of situations that allow such an assessment, however, this cognitive bias would be exceedingly difficult to study in foreign policy decision making. It would almost require a contrived experiment among decision makers or a controlled situation where decision makers were presented the same information in two different ways. Similarly, the range of memory biases or cognitive biases that affect the chances of how fast or accurately one can remember is important, but hard to explore in the study of foreign policy.

Since the cases are handpicked to meet these goals, I don't intend for them to be tests of the importance of cognitive biases. Nor do I claim that the cases are representative of all foreign policy decisions. At the same time, the cases are anchored in the facts, and explanations other than those based on cognitive biases are offered in each case, even highlighted in terms of their gravity. Each chapter tends to focus on one cognitive bias, but some chapters cover more than one. I argue that the Iraq War of 2003 involved decision making marked by the bias of overconfidence, but also by the related bias of overoptimism and by the planning fallacy bias, which is a tendency to underestimate task completion times.[18]

One point is worth making here. This work draws in part on experimental research on individuals. One might question to what extent such research can illuminate foreign policy decisions. Countries, after all, are more than the individuals that run them, and experiments on individuals cannot easily replicate the conditions under which leaders and diplomats must make decisions.

It is important to bear such limitations in mind,[19] but experimental work can be quite insightful and may point us in important directions.[20] While leaders and diplomats act in a different setting than the rest of us, we are all human beings, subject to similar cognitive behaviors. As behavioral economist Dan Ariely puts it, experiments can offer "an illustration of a general principle, providing insight into how we think and how we make decisions—not only in the context of a particular experiment but, by extrapolation, in many contexts of life."[21] This book is not based solely on experimental research. It also draws on my own academic work, and on the excellent work of others on real-world cases of decision making. The combination of approaches should advance understanding of decision making in international relations.

## Conclusion

*National Security through a Cockeyed Lens* illuminates the role of cognitive biases for decision makers who may be subject to them, students and scholars who want to study them, and the layperson who would like to avoid them. By the end of the book, I hope that the reader understands better how foreign policy decisions are made, the biases that may undermine good decision making, and also perhaps how to at least try to avoid these errors as leaders and laypeople. Of course, the book also aims to enhance the reader's understanding of American foreign policy and national security—which should be useful, given that the United States remains the world's leading power. Its citizens and those of other countries would benefit from a better understanding of its decisions and what they have produced in world politics, and of how other actors have seen—and interacted with—the United States.

# CHAPTER ONE

# Afghanistan and Conflict

## Intention and Threat Perception

Some might say that the story of war-ravaged Afghanistan is centuries old, figuring center stage in the lives of empires, great powers, and rogue actors before retreating into isolation. It's certainly true of Afghanistan in the past thirty-five years at least, having endured various factions vying for influence, Islamic extremists competing with pluralists and communists for power, the Taliban fighting Western powers for control, and American special forces and drones targeting al-Qaeda and Taliban forces night and day.

Long before Iraq attacked Iran in September of 1980, triggering the eight-year-long Iran–Iraq War, and Iraq invaded Kuwait in August 1990—well before the shocking terrorist attacks of September 11, 2001, and the U.S.-led wars in Afghanistan and Iraq—an event occurred in world politics that would have a lasting influence on American foreign policy and global security. The Soviets invaded and occupied Afghanistan in December 1979, causing a global response that helped end the Soviet Union and the Cold War, gave rise to al-Qaeda, and put in motion events that eventually led to American and global involvement in Afghanistan and Iraq after the 9/11 attacks.

The modern story of the rise and entanglement of the United States in the Middle East begins in 1979—a year that, as historian David Lesch has noted, shaped the Middle East of today.[1] In understanding this tale, we get a good idea of what helped shape American foreign policy in the region. And, in doing so, we can learn something about the role of cognitive biases in these events.

## Argument: Perception versus Reality

Studies show that individuals and decision makers tend to view themselves as more virtuous and less threatening than others view them. In invading Afghanistan, Moscow saw itself as much less hostile than Washington saw it. While the

Soviet Union might have considered the potential for dominating South Asia and the Persian Gulf in its decision to invade Afghanistan, there is strong evidence that its intentions were far more limited and that it mistakenly believed other countries would not be as concerned by its actions as they turned out to be. In fact, the United States responded quite strongly, perceiving a greater danger than was probably intended despite the shock of the invasion. What transpired in this case is not atypical of other conflict processes in human and world politics.

## Cognitive Biases in Play

A key bias is a tendency to see ourselves as virtuous and to assume that others see us that way, too. Leaders sometimes unintentionally make decisions that other states perceive as threats. Without understanding how others will view and react to their actions, leaders can make poor decisions. Research shows that actors tend to simplify their environments;[2] they assume that if their intentions are good, others will know as much. They assume that others see them as they see themselves, but that assumption is faulty.[3]

As Daniel Kahneman and Jonathan Renshon point out, studies show that not only do people tend to perceive themselves as more virtuous than others see them, but they also see themselves as much less hostile than they view their adversaries and are not well aware of how they appear to others.[4] In October 1950, as coalition forces were moving rapidly up the Korean Peninsula, policy makers in Washington debated how far to advance, attempting to predict China's response. U.S. Secretary of State Dean Acheson was convinced that "no possible shred of evidence could have existed in the minds of the Chinese Communists about the non-threatening intentions of the forces of the United Nations."[5] U.S. leaders considered themselves unhostile toward China, and they assumed that the Chinese felt the same way. Because of this assumption, Washington was incapable of interpreting the Chinese intervention as a reaction to a threat. Instead, Americans saw the Chinese reaction as an expression of fundamental hostility toward the United States. Some historians now believe that Chinese leaders viewed advancing Allied forces as a threat to their regime.[6] It is interesting to consider, as a quick aside, whether similar cognitive dimensions influence modern Sino-American relations and, if so, what can be done to preempt any potential conflict this relationship—which will be critical to world stability in the twenty-first century—might bring about.

Leaders tend to believe that they understand the other side's view of the world, and assume that their messages have been received and interpreted as intended. This supposition predisposes them to believe erroneously that others will view their behavior as less threatening than it is. As Herbert Butterfield puts it, "it is never possible for you to realize or remember properly that since [the adversary] cannot see the inside of your mind, he can never have the same assurance of your intentions that you have."[7] Robert McNamara, secretary of defense under President John F. Kennedy, and former national security advisor McGeorge Bundy were surprised that the Soviets worried about a U.S. first strike during the Cold War, because they knew the administration had no intentions of striking first.[8] For his part, John Foster Dulles was almost certainly wrong when he said "Khrushchev does not need to be convinced of our good intentions."[9]

The tendency to assume that others see us as we see ourselves appears to be fed by two other cognitive biases. The first is the illusion of transparency: individuals often believe that their internal states are more apparent to others than is actually the case. In the domain of public speaking, for example, individuals who are nervous about delivering a speech believe their nervousness is more apparent to their audience than it is.[10] Meanwhile, the second cognitive bias—fundamental attribution error—can undergird the dynamic of seeing others as more threatening, because it leads us to focus attention not on the context of a situation but on the individuals on the other side. As Kahneman and Renshon argue, the fundamental attribution error is one of the most common cognitive failures in conflict situations. Even if we are sure that context, and not characteristics, drives the behavior of others, we still tend to associate a person's behavior with disposition—a tendency that is amplified when we are unsure of what has caused the behavior. During tense interactions between government representatives, for instance, policy makers often attribute the aggressive behavior of the other side to deep hostilities while excusing their own provocations as the result of being "pushed into a corner." Kahneman and Renshon point to World War I, noting that "the leaders of every one of the nations that would soon be at war perceived themselves as significantly less hostile than their adversaries."[11] We can see how such thinking makes compromise more difficult and conflict more likely.

Focusing on context instead might yield explanations for others' behavior that are less likely to center on personality traits and intentions. Islamic radicals could explain the U.S.-led invasion of Kuwait by virtue of the threat Iraq posed not only to Arab states in the Persian Gulf but to the global economy, which depended on reasonable oil prices and predictable supplies. Or, with the attribution error, radicals could see greed, evil, and depravation in America's behavior, independent of some of the contextual complexities, contributing to a profound misunderstanding of the United States and motivating a deranged desire to destroy it.

Robert Jervis has argued that we are likely to see actors as more threaten-ing than they really are and incorrectly label them as defensive when they are offensive, and that this dynamic results partly from a fundamental attribution error. It is not exactly clear what contributed to mutual threat perception among the great powers, but it may have arisen from a variety of psychological factors that in addition to the attribution error include psychodynamic, cognitive, de-velopmental, and social factors.[12] Other work on cognitive factors demonstrates that misperceptions occur in various international relationships, not just those between allies and adversaries,[13] and that they can seriously contribute to threat perceptions.[14]

Cognitive biases of the kind described here can produce real problems. See-ing one as acting in defense when others are threatened creates a dangerous dy-namic. The adversary's response can be perceived as especially aggressive; after all, why would the adversary be so aggressive against an actor who was acting in self-defense or with positive intent? Some studies show that cognitive biases characterized not only relations between America and Iran but also their rela-tions with countries in the Persian Gulf region. As Herrmann and Fischerkeller assert, "neither prevailing American nor prevailing Iranian views recognize the threat the other sees while they both are convinced the other has revisionist intentions."[15]

Under this dynamic we can react in kind, which simply reaffirms others' view that our intentions are not good, thereby pushing them to react against us. A set of poor decisions can take place in this action–reaction dynamic, leaving every-one worse off.

## More Defensive Than Offensive: How Moscow Likely Saw It

Why is it reasonable to believe that the Soviet invasion and occupation of Af-ghanistan, as provocative and brutal as they were, were defensive actions and not offensive or expansionist? First, the Persian Gulf oil fields of Iran and the Gulf states are located on the western edge of Iran while Afghanistan is on its far east-ern edge, with mountainous country lying in between. If the USSR wanted direct or indirect influence over the region's oil, it would have had every reason to go di-rectly through Iranian Azerbaijan, which the Soviets occupied from 1941 to 1946. While strategic blunders are not uncommon in the annals of history, it seems inconceivable that this fact could have been lost on Soviet military planners. It is far more likely that Moscow did not intend such a move in the first place.

For a brief period, Soviet scholarship focused on the possibility that Moscow had legitimate objectives in the Gulf. But the debate was widely considered to be merely academic for many reasons, including the obvious difficulties of executing such an invasion and the absence of evidence that such consideration took place among leadership. In fact, as Anatoly Dobrynin, longtime Soviet ambassador to the United States, pointed out, "no factual evidence in Soviet archives" supports this expansive thesis.[16] To the contrary, historical evidence now makes clear that the Soviet Union was not pursuing a master plan for regional expansionism, as most observers believed at the time; rather, Soviet "objectives in Afghanistan were limited from the start."[17] Gromyko would later stress that the Soviets did not intend to move on the Gulf and aimed only to stabilize a Soviet-leaning leadership in Afghanistan; Western politicians exaggerated that Moscow wanted to "grab Afghanistan for itself."[18]

Second, Moscow was obsessed with securing its border with Afghanistan because it feared that a Muslim resurgence in Afghanistan could affect the huge Muslim population in central Asia. In the months prior to the Afghanistan invasion, a series of events highlighted the potential instability along its southern borders.[19] Afghanistan was becoming an anti-Soviet regime, and Moscow hoped to impose a Soviet-backed government to deal with this problem. Imposing a more sympathetic government was the predominant motive broached in a secret meeting on December 12, 1979, which was dominated by intelligence chief Yuri Andropov, defense minister Dmitri Ustinov, and foreign minister Andrei Gromyko, who formed the heart of the Politburo Commission on Afghanistan; Leonid Brezhnev was present but quiescent in part due to his ailing health.[20] Andropov and Gromyko asserted the importance of maintaining stability in Afghanistan. In Gromyko's words: "Under no circumstances may we lose Afghanistan . . . if we lose Afghanistan now and it turns against the Soviet Union, this will result in a sharp setback to our foreign policy."[21] Rather than seeking to expand to the Persian Gulf, Moscow was desperate to maintain control of a neighboring country.

Moscow had committed itself in stages to the survival of the Kabul regime and saw its prestige as tied to this outcome. Soviet leaders focused on safeguarding a pro-Soviet government, reluctantly deciding to invade Afghanistan only after numerous meetings to discuss the matter over a period of one year.[22] Brezhnev believed there was a "real threat that Afghanistan would lose its independence and be turned into an imperialist military bridgehead on our southern border."[23] Moscow may have been concerned about greater Western involvement in the region.

Third, the record strongly suggests that Moscow aimed to accomplish its goals relatively quickly, after which the bulk of Soviet troops would withdraw from Afghanistan. In their December 12, 1979, meeting, this argument was made by

Ustinov and backed by Gromyko;[24] Andropov at first opposed intervention but then, partly because of his close political alliance with Ustinov, changed course.[25] In January, Brezhnev told Dobrynin with confidence that "it'll be over in three to four weeks," and later in 1980 he raised the prospect of Soviet withdrawal at a Politburo meeting.[26] There is no evidence that they considered the invasion to be a long-term venture or a bridge to other exploits in the region.

Fourth, if Moscow had broader ambitions, it should not have been surprised by international opposition to the invasion. But as I discuss later in this chapter, the U.S.-led reaction to the invasion of Afghanistan did appear to generate surprise and recrimination in Moscow, which only worsened the crisis by pushing the two great powers into what some have called a second Cold War period.

## Acting Offensively: How America Saw It

While there is strong reason to believe that the Soviet Union was focused solely on Afghanistan and considered its actions not to be ambitious or threatening, many others did perceive the invasion as an aggressive act. After the invasion, important decision makers, particularly in Washington, described the act as part of a grand, chess-like scheme and feared that Moscow might even invade the Persian Gulf. When the Soviets invaded Afghanistan, the American policy of détente toward Moscow—trying to engage it in order to contain it—was replaced with an outright return to Cold War considerations in Washington. Even before détente, mutual threat perceptions dominated Cold War thinking in Moscow and Washington.[27]

To be sure, Washington was not unreasonable in worrying about the invasion. The superpowers had a tacit agreement in which Moscow could intervene militarily and control its Eastern Europe sphere of influence, but not beyond this area. The invasion appeared offensive partly because it violated this understanding; was on such a wide scale and brutal; and, as Secretary of State Cyrus Vance saw it, could "set a dangerous precedent for Soviet aggression in other areas."[28] In addition, the Afghanistan intervention took place at a time of Western vulnerability in the Middle East. The region was unstable largely because the U.S. framework for Gulf security collapsed in 1979 with the fall of the Shah of Iran, who had largely supported U.S. security interests in the Middle East and was replaced by the virulently anti-American Ayatollah Khomeini. The Iranian Revolution threatened to spread throughout the oil-producing Middle East, where it could target Arab monarchies like the al-Saud of Saudi Arabia, which was viewed as corrupt, illegitimate, and lackeys of the United States who deserved to be toppled.

From Washington's perspective, the Afghanistan intervention presented the

West with the possibility that Moscow would exploit U.S. vulnerability in the Middle East by invading the Gulf.[29] Its invasion of Afghanistan brought Moscow's troops about 320 miles closer to the Gulf and stoked fears that Moscow might try to gain influence over the Persian Gulf, which lay just beyond Afghanistan. The Russians, it was said, had always wanted a warm-water port as well as influence in the region. The perception of Soviet political and military gains in Angola, Ethiopia, South Yemen, and now Afghanistan, coupled with Washington's loss of Iran as an ally, further damaged U.S. credibility by suggesting that Washington could not stop rising Soviet influence.

After the invasion, U.S. hardliners who espoused geopolitical resolve against the USSR gained precedence over moderates,[30] and the public and Congress significantly bolstered their support of U.S. strategic efforts. Increased public support for defense spending—which was recorded in Gallup polls at the highest point in more than a decade—was clearly related to Afghanistan.[31] Even the generally dovish Secretary Vance provided a glimpse into how Moscow was viewed in Washington. In testimony before Congress on March 27, 1980, he said, "some have argued that a strong response to Soviet military growth and aggression is overreaction. But to disregard the growth of Soviet military programs and budgets . . . or to explain aggression as a defensive maneuver . . . is to take refuge in illusion."[32] For his part, national security advisor Zbigniew Brzezinski viewed the invasion "as ultimate proof of aggressive intent,"[33] confirming what he thought he already knew about the Russians, and he tried to push Washington toward what many considered a hawkish stand.

In January 1980, nine percent of Americans polled favored sending U.S. troops to Afghanistan; a month later, Americans supported the use of U.S. troops to defend other countries against a Soviet invasion by a significant seventy-five percent to eighteen percent.[34] Writing in the aftermath of the invasion, U.S. ambassador to Moscow George Kennan stated that there had not since World War II been "as far-reaching a militarization of thought and discourse in the capital."[35] The Carter administration was committed to a three percent real increase in fiscal year 1981 defense spending, but this budget request was withdrawn in direct response to the invasion of Afghanistan; on January 28 and March 26, 1980, Congress submitted a substantially revised budget calling for significantly higher defense spending. Confronted by the Soviet threat, Carter asked for $157 billion for military expenditures in fiscal year 1981, nearly $20 billion more than in 1980.[36] Congress insisted on even higher spending.

The invasion shocked President Carter, who described it as "an unprecedented act," a "radical departure from the policies or actions that the Soviets have pursued since the Second World War,"[37] and "the most serious threat to the peace since the Second World War."[38] Appearing not to believe that Moscow could do something so provocative, Carter asserted that his opinion of the Soviets had "changed more drastically in the last week than in the previous two-and-a-half years"[39] and sent Brezhnev a message on the presidential hotline claiming that the invasion "could mark a fundamental and long-lasting turning point" in superpower relations.[40]

In Carter's view, a "successful take-over of Afghanistan would give the Soviets deep penetration between Iran and Pakistan, and pose a threat to the rich oil fields of the Persian Gulf area."[41] Shortly after the invasion, the Carter Doctrine was enunciated, committing Washington to protect its interests in the Gulf by military force if necessary. President Carter asserted that "an attempt by any outside force to gain control of the Persian Gulf region will be regarded as an assault on the vital interests of the United States of America, and such an assault will be repelled by any means necessary, including military force."[42] The United States even considered using nuclear weapons to stop a possible Soviet invasion of the Gulf,[43] taking numerous actions to strengthen itself and its allies, to punish the USSR, and to undermine its efforts in Afghanistan by strongly supporting the Afghan rebels. These efforts seriously contributed to Moscow's failure in Afghanistan and hurt its foreign policy interests elsewhere in the world.

Washington accelerated development of the U.S. Rapid Deployment Force (RDF), which delivered massive American force to the Persian Gulf, secured access to military facilities in the Middle East, upgraded the U.S.-operated military base at Diego Garcia in the Indian Ocean, and urged efforts to develop the Saudi military infrastructure for the entry of U.S. forces. These actions helped the United States in its rivalry with the Soviet Union in the Persian Gulf and would later play a critical role in reversing Iraq's invasion of Kuwait in August 1990.[44] As Secretary of Defense Harold Brown stressed, the RDF was not a response to internal matters in the Gulf but was rather intended "to offset Soviet forces."[45] The largest comparative increase in the fiscal year 1981 budget was in airlift and sealift, which reflected the commitment to the RDF.[46]

Beyond playing a role in its funding, the Afghanistan invasion motivated the growth in the RDF's size and configuration and gave it an anti-Soviet role, particularly with respect to Gulf defense.[47] The size and planning of the RDF was based on an actual, albeit unlikely, Soviet invasion of the Gulf.

## Reagan, Afghanistan, and al-Qaeda

America's strong reaction to the Soviet invasion of Afghanistan did not end with the Carter administration. The Reagan administration not only continued Carter's Afghanistan policy but also expanded it into a more global "doctrine."

The so-called Reagan Doctrine included U.S. support to anticommunist resistance movements in Soviet-allied nations in Africa, Asia, and Latin America. President Ronald W. Reagan stated in October 1981 that there was "no way" the United States could "stand by" and allow threats against Saudi Arabia to stop its flow of oil.[48] This statement and others like it became known as the Reagan Doctrine, a U.S. commitment to protect Saudi Arabia against external and internal threats to the Persian Gulf and against domestic threats to the regime. The United States made a tacit agreement to protect the Saudis in the 1940s, and the Carter Doctrine reinforced a commitment to protect the free flow of oil from threats outside the region; now Reagan was elevating the U.S. commitment one more notch. Saudi Arabia would become the linchpin of U.S. security in the Gulf.

In 1982, Reagan's famous "evil empire" speech clearly pitted good against evil in the Cold War struggle, underscoring the embedded and not even implied image that he and so many others had of the Soviet Union. He saw the Afghanistan occupation as further evidence of this evil and therefore sought an opportunity to deal the evil empire a major blow.

The Reagan administration seemed to play up or act on the notion of enemy images more than the Carter administration did. In Reagan's words, it was vital to "pray for the salvation of all of those who live in that totalitarian darkness— pray they will discover the joy of knowing God. But until they do, let us be aware that while they preach the supremacy of the state, declare its omnipotence over individual man, and predict its eventual domination of all peoples on the earth, they are the focus of evil in the modern world."[49]

Like the Soviets, Americans were told repeatedly during the Cold War that they were engaged in a vital struggle with a wily and implacable enemy who was bent on conquering the world and whose values were the antithesis of everything they believed. Scholars have shown that enemy images and ideology played a significant role during the period of Cold War confrontation between the United States and the Soviet Union.[50]

Part of Washington's continuing strong response to the invasion and occupation of Saudi Arabia was an attempt to undermine Moscow in Afghanistan. The Reagan administration supported the Afghan resistance, which believed that evicting the godless communists from Muslim Afghanistan was a sacred duty.

The Afghan resistance included thousands of foreign militants, among them Osama bin Laden. America understandably viewed the conflict in Afghanistan through the prism of the Cold War, and was concerned about a potential Soviet threat to the oil-rich Persian Gulf. On the whole, it is estimated that America committed $4 billion to $5 billion between 1980 and 1992 in aid to the mujahideen, with Saudi Arabia matching that amount.[51]

## The Rise of al-Qaeda

The American and global response undermined Moscow's efforts in Afghanistan, but it also had the unintended effect of contributing to the rise of al-Qaeda. Much of the support that bin Laden and his cohorts received, which eventually helped them build al-Qaeda, came from Saudi Arabia. It established and funded the Ittihad-i Islami faction, which became one of the seven Sunni factions based in Peshawar, Pakistan; in turn, the leader of Ittihad-i Islami would become central in establishing the al-Qaeda training camps.[52]

In essence, Washington wanted to fell the Soviet bear, while Riyadh sought to support the Muslim resistance and to spread its brand of Islam, Wahhabism; their actions fundamentally contributed to Moscow's failure in Afghanistan— what some considered to be its Vietnam. While 250,000 Afghan mujahideen fought the Soviets and the communist Afghan government, it is estimated that there were never more than several thousand foreign mujahideen in the field at any one time. Nonetheless, the number of jihadists who participated in the Afghan movement is reported to have been around thirty-five thousand, coming from forty-three countries in the Middle East, North and East Africa, central Asia, and the Far East.

The Saudis provided critical funding to the Afghan Arabs, which was a smaller part of the resistance run largely by bin Laden and which would form the core of al-Qaeda.[53] Founded chiefly by bin Laden, the Makhtab al-Khidamat (also known as the Office of Order or Afghan Services Bureau) trained and recruited non-Afghan Muslims to join the resistance. In court testimony on February 6, 2001, al-Qaeda operative Jamal al-Fadl, a former bin Laden associate who later turned informant for the United States, asserted that bin Laden "funded the organization."[54]

Little did the Saudis, Americans, or other benefactors know that these Afghan Arabs would form the core of a terrorist group capable of committing the massive atrocities of 9/11.[55] By the end of the 1989 war in Afghanistan, bin Laden consciously wanted to use his fighters for conflicts worldwide. He established al-Qaeda ("the base") as an outgrowth of the Makhtab, and al-Qaeda's worldview began to take shape. Although the notion of launching global jihad was controversial within the movement, he eventually triumphed in promoting it and pushing his distorted view of America as a Muslim-hating, crusading nation. The eviction of Soviet forces in 1989 led bin Laden to say repeatedly that the "myth of the superpower was destroyed," and to "now predict . . . the end of the United States."[56] In one interview, he observed that "God used our holy war in Afghanistan to destroy the Russian army and the Soviet Union, and now we ask God to use us one more time to do the same to America and make it a shadow of itself . . . The Americans are a paper tiger."[57] Testimony of one al-Qaeda operative suggested that bin Laden sought to spread the jihad globally as the next step following the Afghanistan war.[58]

## Surprise at America's Reaction

It seems rather clear that the superpowers saw the crisis in quite different terms. While Moscow certainly understood that its invasion would draw ire from the United States, it appeared surprised at the extent of the reaction, including the substantial support of the Afghan resistance and steps to shore up America's global and Middle East defense. If Moscow had broader ambitions, we would expect that Western opposition to the invasion would not have provoked genuine surprise. In fact, it appears that Soviet leaders were not only genuinely "surprised at the strength of denunciation" by the West but also that they "reacted with tough defiance."[59] As Thomas Watson, former ambassador to the USSR, put it, Moscow's surprise resulted from the fact that it thought Washington considered Afghanistan to be relatively unimportant and would not be "disturbed greatly."[60] As Dobrynin points out, Soviet leadership clearly regarded Afghanistan as within its sphere of influence and believed that invading "was not vital to American interests and moreover did not threaten American interests in the Gulf."[61] Perhaps Moscow underestimated just how vulnerable the fall of the Shah of Iran left Washington and how incapable it was to protect the Persian Gulf with military forces in 1979 when these forces had yet to be created.

Brezhnev went to great lengths to establish that Moscow aimed only to prevent Afghanistan from becoming "an imperialist military bridgehead," a point condemned as false by President Carter.[62] Although Moscow prepared itself for handling the short-term military tasks of the actual invasion, it was not prepared for international or even Afghan rebel opposition.[63] As Dobrynin recalls, Gromyko "underestimated the strength of the reaction . . . No one in our embassy in Washington was asked about possible repercussions, and I was not consulted by Gromyko even though I was in Moscow at the time: he believed that the

American reaction, whatever it might be, was not a major factor to be taken into consideration."[64]

The Soviet Union appeared to misestimate the U.S. response and did not fully understand its extent. It might have considered its actions as having defensive intent, assuming that Washington was simply using Afghanistan as a pretext for anti-Sovietism and for a U.S. military buildup, especially in the Gulf.[65] In a report dated January 27, 1980, the Politburo stated that "the USA, its allies, and the PRC have set themselves the goal of using to the maximum extent the events in Afghanistan to intensify the atmosphere of anti-Sovietism and to justify long term foreign policy acts which are hostile to the Soviet Union."[66] This may have further strained U.S.–Soviet relations and accelerated the defeating cycle of mistrust and reaction.

## Conclusion

Under the pressures of U.S.-led efforts, the Afghan resistance, and their own challenges in Afghanistan, Moscow began to realize that it could not win in Afghanistan. It appeared to recognize by February 1987 that it was incapable of marshaling the forces necessary to win the war and announced its decision to withdraw.[67] But the domestic, regional, and international effects of the invasion had already taken their devastating toll, and many observers saw the Afghanistan conflict as contributing to the fall of the Soviet Union because it bled the country of its resources and forced it to face global opposition of various kinds.

It appears that Moscow generally sought to improve its security by invading Afghanistan to bolster a pro-Soviet government and that it was not its intention to invade the Persian Gulf. However, its action was viewed as highly threatening and pushed the United States and its allies to take countermeasures that made the USSR's security worse than if Afghanistan had not been invaded. This is a classic example of the security dilemma, a famous theory of international relations.[68] According to the security dilemma, any state's attempt to improve its security would under certain conditions decrease the security of other states, pushing them to take countermeasures that may leave the initiating state with no net gain.[69] Underlying the theory are the cognitive dynamics discussed here, making Afghanistan a good case study for students and observers of world politics. Indeed, in the security dilemma, the actor increasing its security assumes that its actions are not offensive and that others will understand as much, when in fact they do regard those actions as offensive. The actor then might mistake their response for aggressive intent, when in fact they think they are protecting themselves from the actor. This case should remind us, and especially leaders, that our self-perception is often much different from how we appear to others. We should be careful not to seem more threatening than we intend to be, because doing so can incite a strong reaction against us.

The Afghanistan story did not end with the Soviet withdrawal in 1989. Rather, this war would bring new stories, including the increasing military role of the United States in the Persian Gulf, the rise of al-Qaeda in world politics, the attacks of 9/11, and the resulting American attempts to restrain transnational terrorism and the Taliban through its own war in Afghanistan, now over a decade old.

It is vital to understand the Afghanistan case not only because it shaped subsequent events, but also because it helps reveal the cognitive biases that are sometimes associated with both human and great power conflict. States often fail to cooperate or, worse yet, engage in various forms of conflict because they misinterpret each other's motives or the extent of threat that they pose to others. Avoiding cognitive bias requires that it be understood in the first place. This classic lesson helps explain the great power conflicts of the past and could help us avoid future conflicts. And it is a lesson that is not only limited to international relations but can also apply to individuals and groups that put their interests in jeopardy by appearing more threatening to others than they intend, possibly leading to dangerous or hurtful countermeasures.

# CHAPTER TWO

# President Reagan and Iran-Contra

## Focus Feature

The conflict in Afghanistan raged right through the presidency of Ronald Reagan, who promised to steel America against the "evil empire" and elevated the national mood with encouraging talk about American power, ideals, and destiny in world politics. But before long, President Reagan would have much more to worry about than just Afghanistan.

Reagan has gone down in history (in the view of some analysts) as one of America's better presidents. He came into office in 1980 at a time when the economy was in shambles, the Cold War was raging, and America's image in the world was in serious doubt. And he appeared to improve some of these problems with a sensibility that Americans appreciated. In fact, Reagan's graceful tonic helped inoculate him against press attacks and gaffes, leading some to believe that he was a Teflon president, immune to life's slings and arrows. Historian Richard Neustadt has argued that the key power of the president is to persuade,[1] and it appears that Reagan knew how to exploit that power abroad and at home.

But there was one event in which the Teflon failed, and Reagan suffered politically: the Iran-Contra affair, in which Reagan and other senior U.S. officials secretly facilitated the sale of arms to Iran. The scandal began as an effort to free seven American hostages held by an Iranian-linked group related to the Army of the Guardians of the Islamic Revolution. Under the plan, Israel would send weapons to Iran, America would resupply Israel, and Israel would then repay America. At least some U.S. officials—and Reagan himself—also hoped that the arms sales would secure the release of American hostages held in Lebanon, since Iran supposedly had some influence over the captors, and would allow U.S. intelligence agencies to fund the Nicaraguan Contras who were based in Honduras fighting a guerilla war to overthrow the Marxist government. At the time, Iran was subject to sanctions, and the U.S. Congress under the Boland Amendment prohibited funding of the Contras. Iran-Contra would prove to be a major fiasco that even Reagan's charms could not damper, although it is unclear to what extent Reagan was aware of the full depth of these multiple strategies.

## Argument: Tunnel Vision

People don't usually make decisions like programmed computers. Instead, they sometimes malfunction in ways that make it harder to produce good decisions. One misstep is to focus too much on one decision-making factor to the exclusion, diminishment, or partial neglect of other equally important or even more salient factors. In this chapter, I argue that President Reagan focused so much on getting the hostages out of Lebanon that he essentially allowed the Iran-Contra affair to become a major scandal. He gave the hostage issue disproportionate importance, and his advisers followed his lead. Getting the hostages out of Lebanon was viewed as so critical that achieving other goals could not compensate for it.

Noncompensatory decision making refers to the notion that foreign policy decisions are often grounded in the rejection or adoption of alternatives based on one or a few dimensions. In the Iran-Contra case, that dimension was the release of the hostages, and the case was not unimportant in influencing future events in the region. It revealed that the United States was in fact supporting Iraq's greatest enemy, reinforcing Saddam's suspicions. It helped convince him that Washington sought to undermine him and could not be trusted—a view that shaped his decisions for years to come,[2] including his decision to go to war in 1991 against the U.S.-led coalition rather than to withdraw from Kuwait.

Before proceeding to the case, I discuss the focusing illusion and noncompensatory decision making, cognitive biases that help explain the Iran-Contra scandal.

## The Focusing Illusion and Noncompensation

The focusing illusion, which is related to and sometimes used interchangeably with the anchoring bias,[3] is a cognitive bias in which individuals place too much importance on one aspect of an event, causing an error in accurately predicting the value of a future outcome, particularly related to happiness. It suggests that when people consider a major life change, they tend to exaggerate how it will affect happiness. We imagine that the result of the change will be either far better or far worse than what actually happens after the dust settles. Daniel Kahneman and David Schkade developed the notion of the focusing illusion, finding it to be responsible for exaggerating the benefits of income to happiness. A rise in income has only a small and transient effect on happiness and well-being, but people consistently overestimate the positive effects of increased pay, partly as a result of a focusing illusion. Kahneman and Schkade suggest that this illusion helps explain why people seek higher incomes beyond a modest threshold (predictions exaggerate the increase in happiness) and why the long-term effect of increased income becomes relatively small (attention shifts to routine tasks).[4] The illusion explains in part how people make mistakes in judging what will make them happy in the future, arising when individuals lend too much credence to the impact of one aspect of their lives on their overall happiness.

Something akin to the focusing illusion is relevant to the study of foreign policy in that it involves excessive focus. We call it noncompensatory decision making. But it also differs from the focusing illusion by highlighting one attribute over others in one decision that we make, rather than life choices related to happiness. Perhaps we let color influence the car we buy or consider the size of a kitchen when purchasing a home. Or, like Jerry on the television sitcom *Seinfeld*, we might judge those we date too narrowly. Jerry always seemed to focus on one attribute that bothered him about a woman that he was dating, whether she had large hands or ate her peas one at a time. And her positive attributes could not compensate for that one lacking feature. Even if she was smart, honest, pleasant, funny, and pretty, he couldn't get over the fact that she ate peas one by one.

Such focusing to the neglect of other attributes allows for noncompensatory decision making. What noncompensatory decision making adds to the focusing illusion is that it explains how it can affect the outcome. The focusing illusion places emphasis on one factor, and noncompensation suggests that it cannot be made up for. Noncompensatory decision making is a notion that penetrates across disciplines and into political science, where it has been applied to foreign policy decision making. To make a distinction, compensatory decisions are rational decisions. They involve identifying the complete set of attributes that are relevant in choosing among options, including both positive and negative impacts. If you wanted to buy a car, for example, you would examine a list of different attributes, ranging from tires to miles driven to the age of the car. You would also assess the relative importance of each attribute and would accordingly compare the options and select the car with the best overall value. In most of our decisions, we compare negative and positive attributes, so that if a car has twenty-five thousand miles on it but is only five years old, the younger age of the car may compensate for the miles driven.

Still, many scholars believe that people just don't have the time to make these assessments. They instead often engage in noncompensatory decisions without evaluating all the attributes and in fact do not compensate for one attribute against another, which allows them to make quicker decisions. Herbert A. Simon famously introduced the notion of "satisficing," in which we select the first adequate option without carefully considering the other options. His idea has spawned a virtual cottage industry of studies. The notion of noncompensatory decision making has much support in the literature, and studies suggest that human beings pursue such approaches under certain conditions. Jorge Arana and Carmelo Leon find that emotions can partially explain this choice among compensatory and simpler noncompensatory decision rules.[5]

Debate exists about the extent to which decisions can still be rational even if they exhibit elements of noncompensatory decision making, but often such decision making threatens rationality. A key characteristic of the noncompensatory principle is that decision makers do not make trade-offs across different dimensions or attributes of a given policy alternative: if an alternative scores low on one dimension, a high score on another dimension will not compensate for it. Decision makers don't sift through information on all dimensions of a given alternative and then do the same for the next alternative. Rather, they focus on one dimension at a time and evaluate their options on that dimension alone before moving on to the next dimension. If an alternative fails to meet the cutoff value on the dimension that is reviewed first, decision makers will not consider any further dimension, rejecting the alternative outright.

Political scientists studying foreign policy have offered many examples of noncompensatory decision making.[6] Alex Mintz and Nehemia Geva have conducted perhaps the most significant work in this area. To them, noncompensatory decision making refers to the notion that foreign policy decisions are "often grounded in the rejection or adoption of alternatives on the basis of one or a few dimensions."[7] If a certain alternative is unacceptable to the decision maker because it fails to meet one goal (such as at the domestic level), then it will be eliminated even if it meets a range of other goals (strategic, for instance). A high score on meeting other goals cannot save that alternative or compensate for its failure to meet the domestic-level consideration. This finding is in contrast to expected utility models that posit a careful consideration of many criteria, or the cybernetic model positing an alternative will be chosen that "satisfices" a certain criteria. It's like rejecting a mate because he lacks ambition in his career, even though you otherwise like him a lot. The predisposition to focus on career aspirations clouds the larger judgment about the person.

There are a number of different ways that decisions can be made in a noncompensatory manner.[8] The goal here is not to exhaust this sometimes technical literature, however, but to offer some sense of the potential impact of this cognitive bias, especially in the field of foreign policy. Which brings us to the Iran-Contra affair.

## Reagan, Hostages, and Mullahs

Ronald Reagan was elected president through a wave of popular support and a virtual landslide victory against Jimmy Carter. Carter entered office quite optimistic and left as an extremely unpopular president who was perceived as having failed on the home front, with the U.S. economy in recession, and on the foreign policy front, with fifty-two American hostages still being held in Iran by Islamist zealots. Not even six years later, Reagan would also have to deal with Iran and hostages, albeit in a different (and nearly disastrous) situation.

The Iran-Contra affair broke when it was disclosed that the United States, in August 1985 and thereafter, had participated in secret dealings with Iran. Through various American officials and foreign actors, the United States had agreed to sell Iran arms, chiefly in exchange for Iran's promise to effect the release of seven American hostages held in Lebanon. The hostages, who were abducted in seven separate incidents between March 1984 and June 1985,[9] were being held by Hezbollah terrorists, over which Iran was believed to have influence.[10] To add to the problem, at some point the policy also stipulated that the proceeds from these sales were to be diverted to the U.S.-backed Contra rebels, who were seeking to overthrow the communist-leaning government in Nicaragua.

## Why Such a Scandal?

The affair assumed scandalous proportions for several reasons.[11] First, although conducted with the knowledge of higher-ranking officials, it was executed in secrecy by what appeared to be lower-ranking National Security Council (NSC) officials. They included Oliver North, who was viewed by some as a person who took the law into his own hands and by others as a great American who risked his career to accomplish important foreign policy tasks. North was a Marine lieutenant-colonel and a middle-level member of the NSC with a flair for grand thinking and patriotism.

The Tower Commission Report, the official investigative report on the affair, depicted these operators as reckless cowboys, "taking control of matters that are the customary province of more sober agencies such as the C.I.A., the State Department and the Defense Department."[12] This was not the ideal reflection of a well-honed policy process, nor was it a particularly astute decision, because it closed out important policy inputs that might have prevented the scandal in the first place.

The controversy was worsened by the fact that, in some measure, U.S. actions ran counter to declared U.S. policies and laws. The United States had declared an embargo on arms sales to Iran and sought to isolate it because of the hostage crisis. As noted earlier in this chapter, the Shah of Iran—whom the United States strongly supported with arms sales in exchange for his proxy role in the region— had been overthrown in the Iranian revolution.

The United States did lift some restrictions on Iran on January 19, 1981, but it maintained the embargo on arms transfers. Selling arms to Iran not only broke the U.S. arms embargo, but also derailed U.S. relations with Arab states, which saw America's actions as hypocritical and not sensible. Arab states had believed that the United States was supporting Iraq in order to keep Iran in check. U.S. officials had stressed this point in high-level meetings with Arab officials in the early 1980s. During his visit to Baghdad in 1983, Donald Rumsfeld told Saddam that the United States was encouraging other nations not to sell weapons to Iran and would continue to do so.[13]

Beyond the problem of breaking its own arms embargo, the U.S. government also had taken a strong stand against negotiating with terrorists directly or indirectly. On January 20, 1984, the secretary of state designated Iran a sponsor of international terrorism, accusing it of involvement in the October 1983 bombing of the U.S. Marine barracks in Lebanon, which killed 243 marines. The United States subsequently pushed other states even harder to stop arms sales to Iran, making the attempt to sell Iran arms for its support in releasing the U.S. hostages doubly problematic: it involved dealing with a terrorist state and appeasing terrorists in Lebanon.

For its part, on December 21, 1982, Congress passed the first Boland Amendment, which prohibited the Department of Defense and the Central Intelligence Agency (CIA) from using funds to overthrow the Nicaraguan government. Later, in October 1984, Congress cut off all funding for the Contras and prohibited any American agency from supporting their efforts. The Iran-Contra affair therefore violated the Boland Amendment and offended some in Congress who had supported the amendment.

## American Motivations

While it is unclear exactly what President Reagan knew about this entire Iran-Contra policy, he knew enough about it to ask why his colleagues supported a policy that violated American law. Why would they put trust in the hands of the Iranians, who had held American hostages for 444 days and declared the United

States an adversary? Why would Washington help Iran when it was more threatening in the region than Iraq?

One reason is that Washington sought to check Moscow. A top secret memo titled "US Policy Toward Iran" asserted that a "dynamic political evolution is taking place inside Iran. Instability caused by the pressures of the Iran–Iraq War, economic deterioration and regime infighting create the potential for major changes in Iran. The Soviet Union is better positioned than the U.S. to exploit and benefit from any power struggle that results in changes in the Iranian regime."[14] High-level officials, including national security advisor Robert McFarlane, had feared that Khomeini might die, triggering a succession struggle in Iran, and that the United States would have no policy or leverage to affect post-Khomeini events in Iran, although the Soviets might.[15]

The American approach aimed to create a strategic opening to Iran, which Colin Powell, then defense assistant to Caspar Weinberger, described as Kissingerian in its proportions.[16] He was not placing it in a rarefied space, but rather underscored just how difficult it would be to execute this strategy. Powell was proud of Weinberger's response to the Iran-Contra strategy, which Weinberger had written across the top of the memo's cover letter containing the first sketch of the strategy: "This is almost too absurd to comment on . . . It's like asking Qaddafi to Washington for a cozy chat," referring to the implacable late Libyan dictator who fashioned himself on anti-Americanism.[17]

For his part, Weinberger praised the policy objective of blocking Moscow's efforts to increase its influence with Iran, but he asserted that "under no circumstances, however, should we now ease our restriction on arms sales to Iran."[18] In his view, a policy reversal "would be seen as inexplicably inconsistent by those nations whom we have urged to refrain from such sales, and would likely lead to increased arms sales by them and a possible alteration of the strategic balance in favor of Iran while Khomeini is still the controlling influence."[19] Secretary Shultz agreed, asserting on June 29, 1985, that the "U.S. Policy Toward Iran" memo exaggerated "Soviet advantages over us in gaining influence," and that "arms supplies from the West are not likely to retard Iranian overtures to the Soviets but could ironically prolong the Iran–Iraq War. Given the disparity in size between Iran and Iraq, this could ultimately mean an Iranian victory, and a fresh burst of energy for anti-Americanism throughout the region."[20]

Despite these concerns, trading arms for hostages was accelerated from March to May 1985. On January 17, 1986, Reagan signed a top secret "finding of necessity" declaring that the covert sale of arms to Iran was in the country's interest.[21] These sales continued even after Iran's major victory at the strategic Fao Peninsula in February 1986. That victory clearly created the specter of Iranian regional domination and threat, as widely perceived in the United States and in the Gulf.

On February 27, 1986, the State Department circulated a briefing memo asserting that after "almost six years, it is clear that the only way to bring Iran to its senses and to the negotiating table is to cut off its munitions."[22] It is not clear from the memo to what extent State Department officials were aware of the full range of the Iran-Contra affair, but a prior memo in May 1986 raised some concern that the arms sales may have funded activities prohibited by legislation.[23]

Still, even if the approach was aimed in part to check Moscow, it certainly did not check Iran, which was the bigger threat in the region. Indeed, Iran won a major victory against Iraq at the Fao Peninsula in February 1986. The attack also put Iran in a position to attack Basra, one of the three key centers in Iraq located about fifty miles from Fao, and threatened to cut off some of Iraq's supply and communication routes. These effects left Iraq at a major strategic disadvantage and could have proved even more disastrous had Iran been able to translate initial victories into more sustained ones.[24]

If Iran had succeeded in taking and holding the Fao Peninsula and then took al-Basra, it would have threatened the vital oil fields of the Persian Gulf and been better able to export its revolution. As one State Department memo noted, an "Iranian victory would be a severe setback for us, and an extremely important event in the Middle Eastern and Muslim worlds."[25] In particular, officials in the State Department feared that the balance in the Iran–Iraq War could be shifting toward Iran, which had been denounced for terrorism.[26]

While the State Department was bemoaning the dangers of Iran's military gains,[27] Iran launched a two-pronged al-Dawa offensive that took the Fao Peninsula on February 9, 1986. Meanwhile, the first five hundred TOW antitank guided missiles were shipped to Iran on February 17 and 18, 1986; another five hundred followed on February 27 while the United States was still considering trading another four thousand TOW missiles; and in October, even more were delivered.[28] Irrespective of their actual military significance—and there are questions as to whether they reached the battlefield in time to influence the Fao attack—there is reason to believe that the Iran-Contra affair strengthened Iran at a time when it was already especially threatening in the region, chiefly by the transfer of intelligence information. As one former NSC official in charge of Iranian affairs put it, the intelligence given to Iran helped the Iranians "gain a more accurate sense of Iraq's defenses," which in turn helped them plan the Fao offensive at the southeastern tip of Iraq, while the TOW and HAWK missiles helped Iran resist the inevitable Iraqi counterattack.[29]

In theory, by co-opting Iran through a more accommodative approach, Washington could prevent Moscow from penetrating Iran and strengthening its regional position in the global balance of power.[30] As suggested earlier in this chapter, the United States at the time believed that Khomeini could be on the ropes, and that a succession struggle in Iran could be in the offing. One of its concerns was that Moscow might capitalize on the situation. One declassified memo stated, "our primary short-term challenge must be to block Moscow's efforts to increase Soviet influence now and after the death of Khomeini."[31] In another memo to the director of the CIA, one official described what became the basis for the arms-for-hostages plan: "Iran has, in fact, now begun moving toward some accommodation with the U.S.S.R. Our urgent need is to develop a broad spectrum of policy moves designed to give us some leverage in the race for influence in Tehran."[32] It continues, saying "the time may now have come to tilt back—at least via our allies—to ensure the Soviets lose . . . potential access to the clergy."[33]

## The Hostages

If America sought to keep Moscow in check, that reason alone could not possibly have driven the Iran-Contra affair. After all, in doing so, it was strengthening Iran in the Persian Gulf at a time when it was considered a greater threat to the region's oil supply than Iraq. Something else was driving this policy. But what could drive Washington into this fiasco and threaten the Reagan administration itself, other than supporting the Contras, which in and of itself was not enough to legitimize such a risky venture?

Evidence strongly suggests that the driving motive of the Iran-Contra case was to obtain the release of American hostages in Lebanon, over which Iran had influence, and to help the Contras in Nicaragua with funds from the arms sale to Iran.[34] The issue of the hostages was especially important to President Reagan. It is not a stretch to say that saving the hostages was the aspect of Iran-Contra that most appealed to Reagan and that centrally drove the policy to the exclusion of other options. Of course, we do not know what Reagan was thinking exactly, nor is it possible to understand what he would have been willing to trade off, even at the cost of not saving the hostages in Lebanon, but we can try to piece together the story.

Multiple sources close to President Reagan noted that he raised the hostage issue on an almost-daily basis, as if he were obsessed with it.[35] The Iran-Contra congressional report concluded that the president was "too influenced by emotional concern for the hostages," which Reagan himself recognized.[36] For his part, Weinberger viewed the trading of arms as an effort by underlings to pander to Reagan, who "wanted the U.S. hostages out of Lebanon."[37] For Weinberger, the president's "very human concern for the safety of the hostages led him to agree with the very bad advice he was getting—that there were some moderate factions in Iran that he could work with, which, of course, was totally untrue."[38] Robert Gates, then deputy CIA director, asserted that there appeared to be "little question that, personally, Reagan was motivated to go forward with the Iranian affair almost entirely because of his obsession with getting the American hostages freed."[39]

Not only was Reagan focused heavily on the hostage crisis, but he also put significant and daily pressure on his subordinates to do something about it.[40] As his frustration mounted over the failure to save the hostages, he became more likely to support the Iran strategy.[41] As Shultz saw it, Reagan bought into the Iran-Contra scheme because he had "such a wish about the hostages."[42]

Defense Secretary Weinberger took notes on December 7, 1985, which can be found in the National Security Archive. First, his notes reveal that President Reagan wanted to free the hostages. Weinberger proceeds to note that he "argued strongly" that arms to Iran would violate American law because the United States had an embargo on such sales, and that Reagan responded by saying that "he could answer charges of illegality but he couldn't answer charge [sic] that 'big strong President Reagan passed up a chance to free hostages.'"[43] One might question if these notes are accurate. It might be that Weinberger wanted a record of his objection to this policy. Even so, there is no reason for him to implicate President Reagan. He could have noted his objections without saying that the president wanted to free the hostages. Or he could have suggested that Reagan had a strategic rationale without painting him as someone who was willing to tolerate illegal actions to free the hostages.

Alas, Reagan may have best described how the crisis evolved when he appeared on national television on March 4, 1987, to address the scandal. He admitted that "what began as a strategic opening to Iran deteriorated, in its implementation, into trading arms for hostages."[44] Perhaps his position on the hostages—whether he tried to impose it on others or others followed it because they knew it was important to him or some combination of the two—altered the evolution of the crisis. The actual dynamics are too hard to discern. Some scholars have even argued that Reagan had the capacity to "convince himself that the truth" was what he wanted it to be, unlike most other politicians. In this interpretation, Reagan was able to make himself believe that he was not trading arms for hostages in Iran, although he later had enough insight to realize that he had.[45]

Some question whether trading arms for hostages was official policy. If not official, perhaps Reagan did not play a direct or indirect role; in other words, perhaps this notion, that his concern for the hostages drove policy, could not be accurate. Evidence shows, however, that the arms-for-hostages scheme was official enough. Although Weinberger thought it was "crazy" to sell Iran TOW missiles,[46] and that he, like Secretary of State George Shultz,[47] was "out of the loop"[48] at some junctures, the plan had high-level support.[49] In a series of classified memos, high-level officials considered the arms strategy beginning in 1984, when the NSC started to exert pressure for a new approach into early 1986.[50] Shultz and Weinberger were alerted to this new potential initiative, but they disapproved.[51] In fact, according to MacFarlane, they met with the president and vice president four to five times in the family quarters of the White House to discuss the arms sales, even though George H. W. Bush would later describe himself as not knowing about the arms deal.[52]

Shultz and Weinberger, who often disagreed, strongly urged President Reagan not to try trading arms for hostages in December 1985 and January 1986, but the strategy nonetheless continued.[53] For his part, Shultz underscored high-level involvement in describing one meeting on the arms initiative, in which it was clear to him by the end of the meeting that the president, the vice president, the director of Central Intelligence, the attorney general, the chief of staff, the national security advisor all had one opinion and he had a different one and Cap shared it. Reagan was not only clearly involved in key aspects of the plan,[54] but he also issued a formal finding authorizing arms shipments to Iran in November 1985,[55] and on January 17, 1986,[56] after having decided as early as August 1985 that the United States would allow such sales.[57]

Reagan may well have been out of the loop on aspects of the approach and tactics. On that score, Shultz wrote during the scandal that Reagan did not grasp the nature of the arms for hostages swaps,[58] while national security adviser John Poindexter contended that Reagan did not know that the proceeds from the arms sales would go to the Contras.[59] Nonetheless, Reagan did appear to be aware of significant aspects of the strategy.

In contrast to popular conceptions of the scandal as a boondoggle conducted by out-of-control underlings in the basement of the White House, the Iran-Contra affair had the imprimatur of high-level officials, and even the secretaries of state and defense knew about it.

## The Train of Time

The U.S.-led invasion of Iraq resulted in the confiscation of millions of pages of records, memos, documents, and transcripts that point to an interesting finding. They show that "Irangate" was not only an important event for U.S. foreign policy but also represented, as I have suggested earlier, a significant change in Saddam's view of the United States. The scandal fed Saddam's mistrust of the United States, with real consequences in the historical process.[60]

As I have shown in my work, various documents suggest that Saddam did not withdraw from Kuwait in 1991, after he had occupied that country in August 1990, partly because he believed that Iraq would have been attacked even if he withdrew as the United States requested. He could not trust the United States to withdraw its forces as it promised if he withdrew his forces.[61] Saddam forced the crisis, and then his own misperceptions contributed to the bad end that he would face.

Events in one time period are often linked to those in another. History cannot be compartmentalized. Moreover, events linked in part by the cognitive biases that shape decision making today can produce outcomes tomorrow.

## Conclusion

The hostage issue was not only important to Reagan and perhaps foremost in his mind, but it was to his advisers, too. They likely read cues from the president and took actions that would be pleasing to him and might have even fulfilled direct or indirect orders from him or his senior staff. It is hard to know to what extent efforts to save the hostages were based on tacit or explicit understandings, but in either case, Reagan's well-known concern about the hostages appears to have played a vital role.

One must ask if the Iran-Contra affair would have occurred were it not for the issue of the hostages. Future thinkers may explore this question in greater detail, but the record presented here seems to suggest that it might not have occurred. Reagan would not have emphasized the importance of releasing the hostages and, in the absence of direct or indirect cues, underlings would probably not have taken such risks in crafting the Iran-Contra plan. One might also ask if Reagan's concern for the hostages was rational. It is a complex question, but it appears that trading arms for hostages might have seemed rational to President Reagan as an individual. That is, in Reagan's own calculations of what mattered, given his individual set of preferences and goals, the scheme might well have made sense. From the standpoint of the United States, however, it might not have been rational—not because Iran-Contra resulted in failure, but because the emotive concerns about the hostages pushed U.S. decision makers to choose a risky option without enough consideration for the costs and benefits of other options.

The other goals of the Iran-Contra mission could have made more sense to the United States in terms of its security and national interest. Pursuing them could be explained effectively by rationalist explanations, but pursuing them in conjunction with trying to release the hostages—and doing it by trading arms—was another matter. If we seek to explain the Iran-Contra affair, it makes sense to draw on both the rational actor and cognitive perspectives. The former provides insight into the motivations that comport with protecting U.S. national interests, while the latter highlights the emotive factors of trying to release the hostages, which played a far larger role in decision making than the rational actor model would predict.

Were it not for Reagan's concerns over the hostages, it is possible that other approaches to Iran, the Contra rebels, and the hostages would have made more sense. Washington, for instance, could have avoided Iran altogether and treated the rebels in Nicaragua and the hostages as separate questions. Or it could have said that America would not yield to hostage taking at all, thus establishing its strength against terrorists and perhaps its global credibility. Rather than trying to cooperate with Iran, it could have reinforced its support of Iraq at a time when Iran was far more threatening and the world was concerned about its possible domination of the oil-rich Persian Gulf. One can imagine a variety of other options. But irrespective of the benefits of these options, they could not easily compensate for the failure to release the hostages, given Reagan's position on the matter. The noncompensatory decision-making bias appeared to be in play and helped drive the crisis down the road to a fiasco. The focus on the hostages meant that other, more reasonable options would not receive due consideration, and that the Iran-Contra option would be harder to consider on rationalist, cost–benefit terms.

# CHAPTER THREE

# Radical Terrorism

## A Cockeyed Lens

-------------------------------------------------------------------------------------

The rise of al-Qaeda can be traced back to the first Afghanistan war aimed at ousting the Soviets. Without that war, it is much less likely that al-Qaeda would have become a transnational terrorist organization. After all, the Soviet invasion brought Osama bin Laden and his "Afghan Arabs" to fight in Afghanistan and contributed to the strengthening of their financing, connections, and infrastructure, and became part of their raison d'être. When the war ended, many fighters returned to their home countries but remained in the terror group, providing it with links around the world that would be exploited to create al-Qaeda offshoots and affiliates.

The rise of al-Qaeda represents one of the more important developments in the past thirty years of world politics, and leaves us with many intriguing, unanswered questions. Why are al-Qaeda and its various offshoots so viciously anti-American? Why do they aspire to kill millions of Americans with nuclear weapons? Why do they and their many sympathizers fail to see that the United States saved Muslims by liberating Kuwait from Iraq's forces or by intervening in Bosnia when almost no other country would? Why do they see nothing good at all in America, even when many of its other adversaries do?

## Argument: Distorted Perception

Osama bin Laden's death did not quell speculation about what drives al-Qaeda and its offshoots to engage in terrorism. Do they hate the American connection to repressive regimes like Saudi Arabia? Are they animated mainly by a resentment of American intervention in the Middle East?[1] Do they loathe freedom and the American way of life, or do they see the United States as standing in the way of Taliban-like states? The list of grievances is long.

There are numerous explanations for al-Qaeda terrorism. U.S. foreign policy and national values are related to the rise of al-Qaeda, but chiefly because American actions are interpreted through al-Qaeda's distorted religious-political perspective. This distorted perspective has various dimensions through which the terror group's leaders are likely to interpret American actions, and it predisposes them to see what they expect to see in American behavior and to view U.S. actions as far more sinister and deliberate than they really are. And therein lies the crux of the problem with radical jihadists.

Al-Qaeda's convoluted view explains why U.S. behavior around the world does not produce massive terrorist acts by other groups. Understanding al-Qaeda's distorted lens sheds light on the phenomenon of al-Qaeda terrorism because it is through that lens that al-Qaeda develops all of its grievances. The lens in turn predisposes its leaders and followers to be subject to two cognitive biases: confirmation bias and seeing patterns that do not exist, captured in some measure by the cognitive bias called the clustering illusion. These two cognitive biases reinforce each other and, in understanding them, we can gain new insights into understanding al-Qaeda's reaction to the 1990–91 Persian Gulf crisis, motivation for the 9/11 attacks, response to the War on Terror and to the 2003 invasion of Iraq, and desire to use nuclear weapons to kill millions of Americans.

## Confirmation Bias: Seeing What We Expect to See

It's hard to make good decisions if we don't accurately interpret the world around us. We might believe that our observations are accurate, but studies show that perception requires an act of judgment by our brains,[2] which can be faulty. Few findings about decision making are more trustworthy than the one that human observations are biased toward confirming the observer's conscious and unconscious expectations and view of the world. Psychologists refer to this as confirmation bias.[3]

Explanations for confirmation bias have varied,[4] but the psychology literature suggests that it arises chiefly when the decision maker seeks information that can confirm rather than disconfirm a hypothesis. Various scholars show that two subjects with opposing beliefs can interpret the same ambiguous evidence as supporting their own position.[5] Experiments have revealed repeatedly that people tend to test hypotheses in a one-sided way, searching for evidence to confirm their hypotheses rather than considering all the relevant evidence. They look for the consequences that they would expect if their hypothesis were true, rather than what would happen if it were false.[6]

Popularizing this notion to explain many of the weird beliefs humans hold, Michael Shermer draws on the best evidence to show that once beliefs are formed, our brain begins to look for and to find confirmatory evidence in support of those beliefs.[7] Experiments have found repeatedly that expectations can influence many things that we do, ranging from whom we date to what type of recreation we most enjoy,[8] to how knowledge of an outcome will then push people to gather information to confirm that outcome.[9]

Decision makers can also ignore or downplay information, data, and ideas that clash with what they already believe. Research suggests that people commonly maintain preexisting beliefs shaped by first impressions, despite dissonant or even contradictory evidence. Psychology professor Philip Tetlock conducted an experiment in which participants viewed evidence from a criminal case and then judged the defendant. Participants received the same information on the case but in a different order. Those who were given the prosecution evidence first were more likely to find the defendant guilty than those who were given the evidence for defense first.[10] Such cognitive biases can emerge in myriad ways and affect how individuals search for and interpret evidence, recall memories,[11] and make basic judgments about others. As Charles A. Duelfer and Stephen Benedict Dyson show in the case of U.S.–Iraqi relations under Saddam Hussein's regime, dissonant information that challenges preexisting notions and clashes with what decision makers expect to see is often discounted, while other information is used to fill in the blanks of what is already believed.[12]

Decision makers may not only confirm or ignore information but may also miss what they don't expect to see, even without any prior beliefs about it. In one of the best-known experiments, psychology professors Christopher Chabris and Daniel Simons asked participants to watch a short video in which six people—three in white shirts and three in black shirts—pass basketballs around. Those watching were asked to keep silent and to count the number of passes made by the people in white shirts. At some point, a gorilla strolled into the middle of the action, facing the camera and thumping its chest, and then left, spending nine seconds on screen. Half of the people who watched the video and counted the passes missed the gorilla. It was as though the gorilla was invisible.[13]

What accounts for this tendency to see what we expect and to miss what we don't? We often appear to prefer information that supports our expectations in negotiations, our outlooks and attitudes, our self-serving conclusions, or our social stereotypes. Prior beliefs lead us to focus on the evidence that supports our belief and to ignore contrary facts.[14] It's like waiting for a friend in a crowd, and mistaking a stranger for that friend. The expectation of seeing the friend causes us to interpret visual information in a certain way, and what we see confirms our expectation.

Like expectations, our desires can also shape what we see. If we want to see something a certain way, it is likely that we will. The notion that love is blind is not just trite but also true. People in love want to see the best in each other and often overlook red flags that others can readily see. Just as we can expect to see something even if we don't want to see it, we can also desire to see something that we don't expect. While these are different mental approaches, they tend to produce a similar result. For instance, when judging the fairness of play in a football game, studies show that fans from both sides overwhelming view the same actions in a different light: they see their team as much more fair than the other. Such studies abound and underscore the power of desire in shaping perception of the world.[15] A variant of seeing what we want to see is that we focus on the options or possibilities that we already like, ignoring or downplaying evidence and goals that clash with our preferences.[16]

Scholars who examined how conflict processes develop have posited the notion of an enemy image. With this prism, all behavior is interpreted to have malign intent, even if it seems cooperative or understanding.[17] Individuals do not judge the behavior of others on its merits, but rather in terms of the actor's supposed nature or character, which skews the evaluation.[18] This bias is so robust and common that, as Kahneman and Renshon point out, social psychologists have dubbed it the fundamental attribution error. The fundamental attribution error can help explain why al-Qaeda views America in evil terms, reinforcing what it expects to see.

The confirmation bias can undermine rationality if it pushes us to exclude options, to restrict the search for novel information, to ignore facts,[19] or to downgrade important information,[20] which can lead to poor decision making and bad outcomes. If we see what we expect and overlook what we don't, we misunderstand our world. Such misunderstanding is certainly a problem for decision makers who are vested with making weighty decisions.

## Seeing Patterns That Do Not Exist

In addition to seeing what we expect to see, we sometimes see patterns and design where they don't exist. Two cognitive biases can cause this phenomenon: the clustering illusion and a bias to favor causal explanations.

The clustering illusion refers to the tendency to erroneously perceive "streaks" or "clusters," caused by a human tendency to underpredict the amount of variability likely to appear in a small sample of random or semirandom data due to chance.[21] A study in 2008 by Jennifer Whitson and Adam Galinsky found that subjects were more likely to report meaningful clusters in semirandom pictures after they had been primed to feel out of control.[22] During the World War II bombing of London by the Nazis, newspapers published maps of where the missiles hit in the city, and citizens saw clusters of strikes and interpreted them as intentional targets. Stories circulated to explain these patterns, including the notion that the Nazis were targeting certain areas to avoid hitting German spies. But later studies showed that there was not anything statistically strange about the distribution of these attacks, and they were not calculated so as to miss hitting spies—something that would be next to impossible to do.[23]

Scholars have shown that human beings have a strong need to make sense of things or to find patterns in what they see. Sometimes the human brain can even prefer a dubious cause to no cause at all, which may explain why we so easily buy into stories of the paranormal. If we can't explain great pieces of architecture like Stonehenge or the pyramids of Egypt, then perhaps they were built by aliens who came to visit us and disappeared. As psychologist Bruce Hood demonstrated in his book *SuperSense*,[24] evidence from cognitive neuroscience now shows that humans readily find patterns and impart agency to them. Subjects watching geometric shapes superimposed with eyes on a computer screen concluded that the shapes represented agents with moral intentions. It is well documented that most people—even those who understand that any result of a series of tosses of a flipped coin is random—make errors in their judgments about random sequences.[25]

It is tempting to reduce the world to something that we can understand and explain. Perhaps we feel more comfortable this way, or perhaps we have not been educated or socialized to think in other terms. After all, many of us hold religious values that emphasize order and design. We are taught that the universe is not random but made by design, and regardless of whether this notion is true, it may influence how we think about our lives in general, even if it only applies in the realm of religion.

One cognitive bias attributable to the search for coherence is a tendency to favor causal explanations. Coherence implies order, so people naturally arrange observations into regular patterns and relationships. If no pattern is apparent, our first thought is that we lack understanding, not that we are dealing with random phenomena that have no purpose or reason. People generally do not accept the notion of chance or randomness. Even gamblers rolling the dice behave as though they exert some control over the roll's outcome.[26] The prevalence of the word "because" in everyday language reflects the human tendency to seek to identify causes.

Seeing patterns in this way—detecting patterns even where they might not exist—may also have been important in terms of human survival. Assume for a moment that you are a Neanderthal. You are walking in the forest when you think you see the outline of a dangerous beast in the shadows, behind the trees. You probably run fast and don't look back, because any error in judgment could mean that you become a predator's snack. But perhaps what you saw was just the rustling of some trees against the shadow of darkening clouds. You ran like mad even though there was no real threat, wasting some energy but getting some healthy aerobics. Now imagine if you looked in the woods, saw some patterns of danger, and ignored them. Ignoring a real threat could lead to your demise, so you might get used to seeing patterns even if they do not exist as an insurance policy against being eaten like a pork chop.

Author and professor Nassim Taleb describes a "triplet of opacity," including an illusion of understanding in which we think we understand a complicated world, and a "retrospective distortion" in which we look back and see history as more organized than it really was.[27] But the design that we seek to impose in retrospect sometimes adds dimensions to the story that did not exist. We *need* to explain things—whether in the social and natural sciences, or art and literature—so we find ways to explain them.[28] Taleb opines that almost no discovery, no technologies of importance have come from design and planning but rather came about from what he calls "black swans"—unpredictable, improbable events that cause major effects.[29] Maybe we are comfortable insinuating design on a mass of behaviors and actions that are somewhat random, somewhat intended, and mixed with a bunch of chaos. We impose a type of backward flow on events to turn them into products of rational, careful design, and to transform them into outputs that were intended and controlled.

The cognitive bias to see patterns where they don't exist can undermine decision making. For instance, we sometimes think that our decisions or the decisions of others have produced the outcomes we observe. Doing so can push us to believe that we are more influential than is really the case, or that others are seeking to undermine us when there is no such pattern in their actions. In turn, we can become overconfident in decision making or more aggressive toward others. At a general level, we can develop blind spots as to the role of others in producing the behaviors that we see.

## Al-Qaeda's Distorted Prism

Al-Qaeda appears to display the cognitive biases discussed in this chapter, but there is another mechanism that makes these biases possible. They are reinforced by al-Qaeda's distortion of Islam and its rigid, ideological worldview. This distortion drives the confirmation bias. It pushes al-Qaeda leaders to see the United States as they expect to see it and to assume that its actions represent a strategy to undermine, humiliate, and control the Muslim world. Arguably, the bias most pivotal to ideological extremism and inter- and intragroup conflict is confirmation bias, the tendency to seek out evidence consistent with one's views and to ignore, dismiss, or selectively reinterpret evidence that contradicts them.[30]

What are the elements of this distorted worldview? One key part is that the foreigner is untrustworthy and non-Muslims are infidels worthy of poor treatment or death.[31] This thought process creates a dichotomy of "us" and "them" and is a natural basis for conflict. Another element is the perception by both Muslims and non-Muslims that the West has sought to impose illegitimate governments. While the separation of church and state is enshrined in Western culture, it is an apostasy for radical jihadists of al-Qaeda's type. Divine authority flows from Allah and Allah alone. Allah cannot be preeminent if temporal, man-made institutions govern fundamental aspects of human life. Dictatorships or tyrannies exercise control over and demand allegiance from the people whose true allegiance can only be to Allah.[32]

It is no mistake that bin Laden describes the abolition of the Ottoman caliphate in March 1924 as an abomination. In a video broadcast on October 7, 2001, bin Laden, appearing with Ayman al-Zawahiri, tried to justify 9/11 as revenge for Muslim pain, observing "since nearly eighty years we have been tasting this humiliation."[33] He evidently referred to the Muslim calendar and the abolition of the caliphate, and to all that it conjured in the minds of radical Islamists, citing it as one of the justifications for the attacks of 9/11. For Turks, Mustafa Kemal Atatürk is a revered figure responsible for initiating economic, political, and social reforms that transformed the former Ottoman Empire into a modern and secular nation–state. Yet through al-Qaeda's distorted lens, he is a traitor, even a devil. For al-Qaeda, Kemal eliminated the center of Islamic community, undermined Muslim unity, pillaged the role of religion in modern life, and mimicked the West.

Radical jihadists also see an unbridgeable divide between the Islamic and Western worlds and want to bring about a confrontation between them. This struggle requires terrorism and martyrdom to liquidate and transform the infidels. In one of al-Qaeda's most important documents, which was either written by or authorized by bin Laden, al-Qaeda justifies aggressive jihad; as Raymond Ibrahim notes, al-Qaeda's aggression has been ultimately rooted in what it believes to be principles intrinsic to Islam.[34] Scholars have noted the religious underpinnings of violence,[35] especially with the most radical jihadists who see the struggle with the West as implacable and maximal.[36]

Al-Qaeda radicalism is built fundamentally on the writings of Sayyid Qutb, who was imprisoned by Egyptian President Gamal Abdel Nasser and executed in 1966, and Hassan al-Banna, who founded the Muslim Brotherhood in 1928 and who sought to oust British control from Egypt, as al-Wahhab had done with regard to the Ottomans in Arabia and as bin Laden sought to do regarding the Americans.[37] The views of bin Laden were shaped by these ideas as well as by those of numerous clerics from various countries, such as Sheik Abdulmajid al-Zindani, a prominent Yemeni cleric who is widely viewed as one of bin Laden's spiritual mentors. The same can be said of Ayman al-Zawahiri. An Egyptian doctor who had been tortured in Cairo prisons for his antiregime activities, he became leader of the Egyptian al-Jihad Group and then became bin Laden's right-hand man.[38]

Qutb emphasized that the West seeks to dominate and destroy the Islamic world and to replace Islam with its own model of how to govern human affairs.[39] Qutb clearly saw Islamic jihad as an offensive movement and went to great lengths to stress this interpretation. In one of his writings, *Jihad in the Cause of God*, Qutb asserted that those who see jihad as defensive are lacking "understanding of the nature of Islam and its primary aim."[40] He emphasized a world divided into the dar-al-Islam (House of Islam) and the dar-al-Harb (House of War), a world divided between believers and unbelievers, and while his writings appeared to be measured and philosophical, his message was clearly divisive, confrontational, and aggressive against the nonbelievers.[41] Al-Qaeda documents and statements are littered with a similar Manichean worldview. In one prominent essay, "Loyalty as Enmity," al-Zawahiri lays out a black-and-white world of infidels and believers and describes 9/11 as the peak of the struggle between infidels and the Islamic Ummah.[42]

Martyrdom is critical to the jihadists' cause, and infidels deserve no better way to die, especially given their designs on the Muslim world. Qutb viewed martyrdom as the highest calling and a great honor and emphasized its importance.[43] Not surprisingly, al-Qaeda has justified martyrdom at length, sometimes twisting the sayings of the prophet Mohammad in lengthy essays on the subject.[44] The Koran says that to die for one's faith is the highest form of witness to God, but it does not extend to martyrdom in suicide attacks. Islam prohibits suicide but, as John Esposito points out, martyrdom is not considered suicide by its proponents, thus getting around this prohibition.[45] Interpretation and distortion are key. Al-

Qaeda distorts the Koran to promote violence. Its messages draw heavily on religious verses and passages that command Muslims to attack the infidels.[46] Al-Qaeda leaders convince their disciples that great rewards await them in heaven, with the pain and sorrows of life replaced by the eternal bliss of paradise and marriage to seventy-two beautiful virgins.

One of bin Laden's central teachers and co-jihadists in the Soviet war in Afghanistan, Abdallah Azzam, asserted that holy war or jihad was "every man's duty" in the event that foreigners took Muslim lands.[47] Jihad against the West for purposes of liberating an oppressed Muslim world was a religious duty, and only force would allow the Ummah to gain victory; for him it was "jihad and the rifle alone: no negotiations, no conferences, and no dialogues."[48]

Al-Qaeda also advances a colonial narrative. The American-led West is seen as composed of powerful, sometimes-colonial countries dominating weaker actors in the Middle East. Al-Qaeda threads its statements with anticolonialism. One of its most involved documents asserts that "Muslim countries today are colonized," either in a "direct or veiled" manner, and that "the real ruler is the Crusader United States."[49] The colonial narrative is prominent enough that al-Qaeda's leaders as well as many leaders in the broader Middle East not only appear to filter the world through it, including American foreign policy behavior, but also use it to sway public opinion throughout the world. President Saddam Hussein, in trying to win support during the 1990–91 Gulf crisis, repeatedly appealed to anticolonial sentiment."[50]

## Seeing What al-Qaeda Expects to See: Confirmation Bias in Play

Fitted with this distorted lens, al-Qaeda leaders see American actions in the Middle East and in the so-called "War on Terror" as sinister and unchangeable. And the lens itself contributes to confirmation bias.

### *The 1990–91 Gulf Crisis*

When U.S.-led forces went to Kuwait to save it from Iraq's invasion, the Saudis and Kuwaitis applauded the effort, which certainly saved the Kuwaiti regime and many Muslims from subjugation or worse. The United Nations also supported it, as did numerous Muslim and non-Muslim countries that joined the coalition, and few countries seriously criticized the U.S.-led effort. Even the Soviet Union ultimately supported American-led efforts against its former ally Iraq, even if grudgingly.

But al-Qaeda's leaders saw it as an abomination. Why? Because they viewed it through an entirely different prism of interpretation. To them, it represented the West's effort to dominate and humiliate Muslims, to continue a crusader movement in the land of Mecca and Medina, and ultimately to steal oil and suppress the Muslim world. They saw it through an extreme religious–political prism that did not allow for nuance or even broad-brush recognitions of complex reality. Through their distorted lens, they saw what they expected to see.

Al-Qaeda's reaction was much less about what the United States and its allies did than about the screen or filter through which its leaders perceived these actions. In fact, everything the United States has done in the Middle East has been viewed as an effort to control the region and its peoples in the form of an old, imperialistic empire. The notion of the West seeking to dominate locals includes in particular the exploitation of the region's land and resources, animating al-Qaeda in the extreme, although it has also resonated in smaller doses throughout the rest of the Muslim world.[51]

## Infidels in the Land of Mecca and Medina

The 9/11 attacks will be studied for decades, and we will learn much more about them. Given what we already know, it appears that a wide range of factors motivated these attacks.[52] The U.S. presence in the Persian Gulf, however, as seen through al-Qaeda's lens, appears to be the most important motivation. The 1990–91 Persian Gulf crisis would ignite one of bin Laden's chief grievances. Seeing the world a particular way, bin Laden repeatedly asserted that it is "not permitted for non-Muslims to stay in Arabia."[53] We should note that the United States was reluctant to go to the Persian Gulf in the first place, with the public and Congress split on the matter. When American troops took positions in the kingdom, they never entered Mecca and Medina and were isolated from Saudi society for fear of offending some of its citizens. Leading Saudi religious scholars not holding bin Laden's extremist views or beholden to the House of Saud also gave their imprimatur to American military deployment. And the American intervention helped Muslims in Kuwait who were besieged by Saddam Hussein's troops.

The Saudi acceptance of U.S. forces and their strategic alliance with Washington strongly motivated bin Laden and other Saudis who opposed the regime.[54] Occupation of Arab land played a key role,[55] as did Saudi rejection of bin Laden's well-known entreaties to have his Afghan rebels protect the kingdom from Saddam instead of the infidels of the West.[56] Since at least 1992, bin Laden had focused his attention on challenging the United States, suggesting a direct connection to the Gulf War. In Afghanistan, to which he had fled from Sudan to take refuge under Taliban rule, he wrote a vitriolic statement—despite the fact that he had no authority, at least under any of the conventional schools of Islam—issuing a fatwa.

Bin Laden's "Declaration of Jihad against the Americans Occupying the Land of the Two Holy Places" appeared in August 1996. Still influenced heavily by the Gulf War, his rejection by the al-Saud regime, and his eviction from Sudan under American pressure, he evidently focused on Saudi Arabia and the United States. In the main, he asserted that to "push the enemy—the greatest *kufr* [infidel]—out of the country is a prime duty. No other duty after Belief is more important than [this] duty . . . Utmost effort should be made to prepare and instigate the Ummah against the enemy, the American–Israeli alliance."[57] In his second paragraph, following typical praises for Allah, he asserted that the "Arabian peninsula has never since Allah made it flat, created its desert, and encircled it with seas been stormed by any forces like the crusader armies spreading in it like locusts, eating its riches."[58] After describing a variety of aggressions against the Muslim world by the Zionist–Crusader alliance, the declaration referred to the occupation of the "two holy places"—a reference to Mecca and Medina—as the most serious transgression of all.[59]

Bin Laden issued another fatwa in February 1998 under the banner of the "World Islamic Front for Jihad against Jews and Crusaders." This fatwa again highlighted what appears to have been bin Laden's chief grievance against his two main targets: the United States and Saudi Arabia. The fatwa lambasted the Saudi regime for allowing infidels to occupy the most sacred lands of Islam, asserted that America had declared war on Allah and on Muslims, and called on the faithful to attack American interests.[60]

## The War on Terror

The 9/11 attacks triggered the U.S.-led War on Terror. Radical jihadists such as those in al-Qaeda have viewed the War on Terror as a war on Islam, even as they tried to exploit it for recruiting and propaganda purposes. Many in the Muslim world also saw the War on Terror as a U.S.-led war on Islam.[61] In fact, in a 2004 Zogby International poll, political scientist Shibley Telhami discovered that more than three-fourths of respondents in Egypt, Jordan, Saudi Arabia, Morocco, Lebanon, and the United Arab Emirates believed that American aims in Iraq were intended in part "to weaken the Muslim world,"[62] with dominating the oil industry as one vehicle for this goal. Muslims polled over the period 2001–8 as part of the Pew Global Attitudes Project had an aggrieved view of the West. Majorities in many Muslim nations—and in some Western European countries, too—believed America's War on Terror to be an effort to control Mideast oil or to dominate the world.[63]

While seeing the War on Terror as a religious threat, al-Qaeda has also welcomed it, as it provides a trigger for conflict between Islam and the West. Al-Qaeda's actions indicate that it has sought to strike up this clash of civilizations, to agitate the audience to its cause, and to win the hearts and minds of the Muslim street.[64] Following the 9/11 attacks, bin Laden noted in a mid-November video that "the number of people who accepted Islam in the days that followed the operations were more than the people who accepted Islam in the last eleven years."[65] Perhaps Qutb influenced al-Qaeda leaders to see the war on terrorism as a clash of civilizations. Qutb certainly sought to spur civilizational conflict, as reflected in a chapter entitled "Islam Is the Real Civilization" in his famous book *Milestones*, and by his repeated references to the superiority of Islam, the depravity of Western civilization, and the need for jihad against the West.[66]

## The 2003 Invasion of Iraq

Al-Qaeda saw the invasion of Iraq, like the 1990–91 Gulf crisis, partly as an effort to dominate Muslims and to steal their oil. As bin Laden put it, after Iraq, the crusader alliance will move to occupy the "rest of the Gulf states to set the stage for controlling and dominating the world. For the big powers believe the Gulf and the Gulf states are the key to controlling the world due to the presence of the largest oil reserves there."[67] In his "Message to the American People," bin Laden asserted that George W. Bush invaded Iraq because he was "blinded" by "black gold," giving priority to "private interests over the interests of America," and leaving himself "stained with the blood of all those killed on both sides, all for the sake of oil and the benefit of private corporations."[68]

Bin Laden's view of Iraq was captured in part in an exchange with Abu Mus'ab al-Zarqawi, who the international media identified as the senior representative of global jihad in Iraq. In February 2004, he sent bin Laden a letter, which American forces later obtained. In it, Zarqawi suggested that Iraq could replace Afghanistan as the new "land of jihad." He called for a civil war in Iraq in order to sabotage American interests in the region, and suggested a deal in which bin Laden would recognize Iraq as the principal land of jihad and, it is implied, Zarqawi would pledge his loyalty to bin Laden. Evidently, bin Laden accepted. On December 27, 2004, he released a tape in which he declared the unification of his group and "the prince, the warrior, and the respected friend, Abu Mus'ab al-Zarqawi and the groups that have joined him, who are the best of the sect fighting for the word of Allah . . . We in al-Qaeda very much welcome your unification with us."[69]

It appears that the Iraq War increased al-Qaeda's concerns about America trying to dominate regional oil and possibly about its close ties to Riyadh. Al-Qaeda launched attacks on Saudi oil facilities in conjunction with the initial phases of the U.S. invasion of Iraq. Al-Qaeda's portrayal of oil-stealing Americans permeated al-Qaeda statements[70] and resonated more broadly, as well. One survey conducted in six Arab states in late February 2003 showed that more than eighty percent of respondents believed that dominating oil was an important motivation for America's invasion of Iraq.[71] Such a view may help explain why polling data in a seventeen-nation survey conducted by the Pew Foundation showed that the Muslim public was somewhat more inclined to support suicide bombings when carried out against Americans and other Westerners in Iraq than in other places.[72]

## Using Nuclear Weapons

Driven by a distorted view of the world and of American foreign policy, al-Qaeda worked hard to obtain nuclear capability and intended to use it on millions of American citizens, if it ever had the chance, and bin Laden declared in 1998 that it was a "religious duty" to acquire weapons of mass destruction (WMD).[73] American forces recovered numerous documents from al-Qaeda houses in Kabul soon after it fell in November 2001 to Northern Alliance forces allied with Washington. They demonstrated that al-Qaeda was pursuing a sophisticated biological weapons program and was certainly seeking to build and deploy a low-grade "dirty" nuclear device; the evidence suggests that it had also sought to develop or acquire a nuclear device.[74] This goal was confirmed by captured al-Qaeda leader Abu Zubaydah, who among other things told American interrogators in April 2002 that al-Qaeda had been working aggressively to build a dirty bomb.[75]

Not only had al-Qaeda sought WMD, but it appeared to be quite willing to use them in massive attacks. Richard Myers, chairman of the U.S. Joint Chiefs of Staff from 2001 to 2005, who had access to secret intelligence on al-Qaeda's WMD plans, described al-Qaeda as ruthless, relentless, and bent on using nuclear and biological weapons to do away with America's way of life.[76] In 2002, al-Qaeda spokesman Sulaiman Abu Geith posted on the Internet that al-Qaeda had the right to punish America for its oppression of Muslims by killing "four million Americans—two million of them children."[77] This notion was backed by a fatwa from a fugitive Saudi cleric who was later arrested by Saudi authorities; just how many Western infidels should be killed became a normal topic of conversation in radical circles.[78] But it had not been the case until around May 2003, when al-Qaeda received some Islamic grounding to justify attacks on Westerners in the form of a treatise issued by a Saudi cleric named Sheikh Nasir bin Hamid al-Fahd. He noted that some estimated the number of Muslims killed directly or indirectly by America at nearly ten million, and that it was permissible for Muslims to enact revenge on non-Muslims.[79]

Why do these jihadists think that killing four million Americans is a positive thing? Through their prism, it makes sense. They do not see American men, women, and children as innocent citizens but rather as frontline, un-Islamic soldiers in service to a vicious empire. Americans are infidels and not Muslims of the right stripe. They are part of the crusader state that wants to pillage and humiliate Muslims and that has destroyed their interests and sought to steal their oil. Killing them will produce justice and might hinder future crimes against Muslims by the Zionist–Crusader alliance, which clearly has joint plans to undermine and then overtake the entire Muslim world. That's the grand strategy that Israel and America share and aim to bring about. In the battle between good and evil, al-Qaeda and its followers are good, with Allah on their side against the scheming, demonic Jews and Christians. Using that rhetoric, killing millions of America makes sense. Through a distorted lens of this proportion, which pushes one to see what it expects to see, the infidels are cosmic enemies that must be destroyed.

## Conclusion

We now accept as a part of our modern lives that al-Qaeda is a terrorist organization that seeks to destroy the United States and Western forms of democracy and capitalism and to replace them with a Taliban-like religious autocracy. But we don't do enough to ask how al-Qaeda could develop such a warped and violent view of the United States. Some people argue that America, poverty, or other social issues are to blame. There may be some truth to a variety of explanations, but there is another reason: al-Qaeda has a warped view of American actions, which drives its cognitive biases. Its leaders don't see the world the way it is; they see the world in a way that they expect and want to see it. Their religious and political lens causes these distortions, which then frustrates, humiliates, and angers them to the point of determined hatred and violence.

If we employ the idea of a distorted prism and cognitive biases, we can see that al-Qaeda and its various affiliates and offshoots see the world through a cockeyed lens. We can also see that American actions are not much to blame. But how others regard them is the key. The United States is often criticized for not understanding the Muslim world or countries and peoples within it. And sometimes this criticism is on target. Americans are not well known for their deep understanding of world politics, economics, and cultures. But what we hear far less is how elements in the Muslim world view the United States. On that score, I argue that part of the divide is that al-Qaeda fundamentally misinterprets American behavior through its distorted lens, and that some of the ideas that it holds are more widely shared in the Muslim world.

Of course, this is not the whole story. The West has engaged in some provocative behavior in the Middle East. Numerous global, regional, and domestic events have combined to contribute to the al-Qaeda pathology, as jihadists and their sympathizers viewed these events through a cognitive lens. We need to understand this lens if we are to have a chance of understanding and then eliminating al-Qaeda.

As the studies discussed here suggest, the problem is not limited to al-Qaeda, although al-Qaeda represents an extreme form of it. How Muslims more broadly view America is important to consider. One of the most significant findings of polling conducted by the Program on International Policy Attitudes is that across the four Muslim countries polled, eight in ten people polled believe that the United States seeks to "weaken and divide the Islamic world."[80] Might this result be explained by the cognitive bias of seeing what we expect to see?

# CHAPTER FOUR

# *The 2003 Invasion of Iraq*

## A War of Overconfidence

From the Greek tragedies to Shakespeare to the real world of fallen leaders, over-confident individuals have sometimes met difficult, even tragic, endings. Over-confidence has been linked to various problems big and small in world politics, including failed diplomacy and war.[1] Since overconfidence is a ubiquitous aspect of the human condition, exploring it should be of wide interest.

This chapter explores the question of overconfidence in American decision making during the 2003 U.S.-led invasion of Iraq. If the Soviet war in Afghanistan of the 1980s contributed to the rise of al-Qaeda, and if the 2001 War in Afghanistan was launched to destroy the Taliban and al-Qaeda after the terrorist attacks of 9/11, the 2003 Iraq War sought to oust Saddam Hussein's regime and continued the linkage of events in history's train.

Operation Iraqi Freedom was launched against Iraq on March 19, 2003, with a massive air attack. Saddam would soon fall, leaving some to wonder whether the birth of a new Middle East was on the horizon. But his demise hardly ended the story of Middle East instability. Washington faced a tortuous challenge in rebuilding Iraq, marked by enormous costs in lives, time, and treasure.

## Argument: Overconfident Actions, Disastrous Results

This chapter provides perhaps the most comprehensive analysis of overconfidence and its causes in the 2003 invasion of Iraq. In exploring the Iraq case, I make two arguments. First, the decision to invade Iraq is a good example of overconfidence and offers a central illustration of this cognitive bias, although the decision to invade Iraq was driven by far more than overconfidence, which plays a part in a much larger story. American decision makers were not overconfident about U.S. capabilities but about the case for going to war and its chances of success. Some might argue that other administrations would have also been similarly overconfident, but that does not appear to be the case. Many observers made the mistake of assuming that Iraq had WMD, and the administration had evidence to support that assumption, but there were quite a few critics who raised red flags about successfully trying to stabilize Iraq. Second, I argue that overconfidence occurred due to a mix of factors: information problems, a weaker-than-usual role of the national media, post–Cold War American global dominance, misplaced analogies, and President George W. Bush's disposition and decision-making style. None of these factors independently would have likely produced overconfidence, but when considered together, they seemed to.

In this chapter I first define overconfidence and discuss what we have learned about it, which allows for a sensible analysis of the Iraq case. I then discuss the administration's goals in invading Iraq and explore to what extent the administration was overconfident. The chapter ends with a discussion of the key factors that fed overconfidence.

## What Is Overconfidence?

Overconfidence is one of the most reliable findings in decision making. It is defined differently by scholars in various disciplines, but is generally viewed as a bias in which someone's subjective confidence in their judgments is reliably greater than their objective accuracy. In particular, it can fairly be described as the overestimation of the accuracy of one's views, actual capability, and chances of success. The international relations literature focuses far less on the accuracy of views and instead refers to overconfidence with respect to (1) the overestimation of capabilities and (2) the chances of success.[2] I evaluate the U.S. approach to decision making in the Iraq case in terms of these two aspects of overconfidence.

Not all scholars believe that individuals have a tendency to be overconfident,[3] and many would argue that we must examine the conditions of decisions in order to interpret when and if overconfidence exists.[4] Some would say that it is just as important to understand the phenomena of underconfidence, or of overestimating the capabilities of others.[5] Even so, the findings on overconfidence are fairly wide ranging.[6] As Don Moore and Paul Healy document, researchers in multiple disciplines over the past three decades have offered overconfidence as an explanation for a variety events, including wars, strikes, litigation, entrepreneurial failures, and stock market bubbles.[7] As the behavioral economist Dan Ariely puts it, everyone, except the deeply depressed, overestimates the chances of things like obtaining a raise, staying married, and getting away with parking illegally. But of course even the people who go into marriage with a positive outlook may end up divorcing.[8]

An exaggerated view of one's capabilities can be problematic in many walks of life. Terrance Odean has shown that overconfident investors—those who feel that their knowledge capabilities about stocks are greater than they actually are— trade more and have lower returns,[9] and that buying a basic index fund of hundreds of stocks would have beat the performance of fund managers fifty to eighty percent of the time in the 1970s, 80s, and 90s.[10] One analyst went so far as to say that "a blindfolded chimpanzee throwing darts" at a board of stocks could pick the winners just as well as the Wall Street pros, despite their significant overconfidence about their own performance.[11] Studies typically report views of exaggerated capabilities, such as one in which sixty-seven to ninety-six percent of people rated their own qualities as better than those of their peers.[12] Studies show repeatedly that we believe that we are smarter than we are. Professors of psychology Justin Kruger and David Dunning found that students who scored in the bottom quartile on tests of humor, logic, and grammar grossly overestimated their test performance and ability. Test scores put these students in the twelfth percentile, but they estimated themselves to be in the sixty-second percentile. Meanwhile, people with true knowledge tended to underestimate their competence.[13]

An exaggerated view of capabilities can feed into the second central dimension of overconfidence: overestimating our chances of success.[14] Political scientist Dominic Johnson argues that overconfidence contributes significantly to war by pushing leaders to think erroneously that they can win. He believes that overconfidence is an engrained genetic trait that might once have been helpful in war and conflict. He suggests that on the ancient African savannah, it was actually rational to misestimate your own capacities: a fearsome appearance and bold tactics could intimidate the enemy and could help carry the day during lightning raids on enemy camps. But today, given modern weaponry, bureaucratic planning, and mass armies, a cocky disposition is as likely to be problematic as glorious. In other words, military overconfidence is a psychological holdover—a cognitive appendix—from an earlier period in human history.[15]

Being less smart than we think may also help explain why we cannot make predictions as well as we think we can.[16] Human beings have always sought to predict the future, and we have usually been wrong. In one set of interesting experiments, people who knew how events actually transpired falsely overestimated the probability that they would have predicted them.[17]

Overconfidence can affect a range of actions in international relations, including planning, which is known as the planning fallacy. People often think they will accomplish a goal much sooner than it turns out, including leaders who have taken their empires, city-states, dukedoms, and countries to wars that turned out to be surprising disasters. Technically speaking, the base rate fallacy or base rate neglect results when we assess the probability of some hypothesis given existing evidence without taking into account the evidence of other cases outside our particular case.

The so-called planning fallacy is an example of a problem in which base rates are not given in numerical terms but must be abstracted from experience. In planning a research project, for example, one may estimate its completion taking ten days. This estimate is based on relevant case-specific evidence: desired length of report, availability of source materials, difficulty of the subject matter, allowance for both predictable and unforeseeable interruptions, and so on. One continues to ignore the noncausal, probabilistic evidence based on many similar projects in the past.

## Why the United States Invaded Iraq

Before examining the U.S.-led invasion of Iraq in light of the question of over-confidence, it is important to provide a brief background on the Iraq case. Among other things, doing so allows for comparing the outcome of the invasion against its goals.

One of the major claims against Iraq is that it had defied sixteen United Nations (UN) resolutions passed between 1991 and 2002, starting with UN Security Council (UNSC) Resolution 687, which was the most important. This post–Gulf War 1991 resolution mandated full disclosure of all of Iraq's ballistic missile stocks (above a range of 150 kilometers) and production facilities, all nuclear materials, chemical and biological weapons and facilities, and cooperation in their destruction. Paragraphs 10 through 12 required Iraq to "unconditionally undertake not to use, develop, construct, or acquire" WMD. UN Resolution 687 also forced Iraq to accept the UN-demarcated border with Kuwait, the sovereignty of Kuwaiti territory, and UN peacekeepers on the Iraq–Kuwait border.

In the wake of 9/11, the Bush administration refocused attention on Iraq. In President Bush's speech to the UN on September 12, 2002, he demanded that Iraq comply immediately with the previous sixteen UN resolutions. He claimed that because Iraq was continuing to pursue the acquisition of WMD and missile delivery systems, it represented a "grave and gathering danger" to American and global security. And he pointed out that the UN had struggled with Iraq for a dozen years to ensure its compliance with the demands of UN Resolution 687, and that Iraq defied its wishes, creating a crisis of credibility regarding UN resolve. He held out the prospect that UN inspectors could find Saddam's WMD, but he also asserted that the United States was willing to act unilaterally, observing that it is not possible to "stand by and do nothing while dangers gather."

The administration was clearly highly concerned about future attacks on the American homeland. Future research may reveal that the 9/11 attacks triggered the most primitive emotions of fear within the administration and country—possibly representing additional cognitive biases in play—which could help explain why the media, public, and politicians in both parties largely didn't question the decision to invade Iraq.

Washington pushed hard to pass a seventeenth resolution against Iraq on November 8, 2002. Resolution 1441 required Baghdad to admit inspectors from the UN Monitoring, Verification, and Inspection Commission and from the International Atomic Energy Agency and to comply fully with all foregoing resolutions. The resolution, which was passed unanimously by the UNSC, declared that Iraq "has been and remains in material breach" of its obligations under previous UN resolutions; gave Iraq thirty days to declare its WMD to the UNSC; and emphasized that false statements would constitute a further "material breach," for which Iraq could face serious consequences. The resolution suggested the use of force against Iraq if it committed a "material breach" or serious infraction in its cooperation with efforts to identify and destroy its WMD capability, but the notion of a material breach was interpreted differently among UNSC members.

For its part, Iraq moved to comply with Resolution 1441 by allowing UN inspectors back into the country and by submitting to the UN twelve thousand pages and several compact discs supposedly describing its weapons capabilities. Baghdad claimed that it lacked WMD programs and had no WMD in storage. Unfortunately, these disclosures were thought to be incomplete. Partly as a result of this skepticism and partly because Iraq was seen as not meeting the conditions of UN Resolution 1441 or previous UN resolutions, the United States and Britain drafted an eighteenth resolution against Iraq that essentially called for war. The two countries offered somewhat different justifications for war, but in essence they were both convinced that Iraq's violation of the previous seventeen UN resolutions gave them sufficient basis for using force.

In the absence of yet-to-be released documents, only a sensible sketch of the key reasons for going to war is possible. This analysis won't include more complex factors such as group dynamics, domestic political considerations, and the impact of analogies. Nonetheless, these factors appear to be three of the central motivations.

First, the United States was concerned about Iraqi WMD programs. On August 14, 2002, national security adviser Condoleezza Rice chaired a meeting that laid out U.S. goals in Iraq in a draft of a national security presidential directive titled "Iraq: Goals, Objectives, and Strategy." President Bush signed the directive, making it official policy, on August 29. The document emphasized Washington's desire to overthrow Saddam Hussein's regime in order to eliminate its WMD, to end its threat to the region, and to create democracy in Iraq. In June 2001, the CIA reported that although the evidence was not fully clear, it appeared that Iraq had used the period between 1998 and 2001 to rebuild prohibited WMD programs. In October 2002, a special national intelligence estimate more clearly articulated those accusations: "Iraq has continued its weapons of mass destruction programs in defiance of UN resolutions and restrictions. Baghdad has chemical and biological weapons as well as missiles with ranges in excess of UN restrictions; if left unchecked, it probably will have a nuclear weapon during this decade."

In one key document, President Bush warned that if the Iraqi regime were "able to produce, buy, or steal an amount of highly enriched uranium a little larger than a single softball, it could have a nuclear weapon in less than a year."[18] In September 2002, he cited a British intelligence report indicating that Iraq could launch a chemical or biological attack forty-five minutes after the order was given.[19] The administration also described Iraq as capable of using WMD against the United States, a position that was not shared by the intelligence analysts who wrote the October 2002 national intelligence estimate.[20]

The attacks of 9/11 raised the stakes enough that the administration felt it could not tolerate WMD in a dictator's hands, especially one with Saddam's record of aggression. Vice President Dick Cheney asserted in August 2002: "If the United States could have preempted 9/11, we would, no question. Should we be able to prevent another, much more devastating attack, we will, no question."[21] From this perspective, irrefutable facts about Iraq's capabilities and intentions were unnecessary; Saddam had given the administration enough reason to have serious doubts about his intentions in a post-9/11 environment. As Bush asserted in his January 28, 2003, State of the Union speech, a "brutal dictator, with a history of reckless aggression, with ties to terrorism, with great potential wealth, will not be permitted to dominate a vital region and threaten the United States."[22]

The Bush doctrine of preemption was articulated in the State of the Union address on January 29, 2002, and then formally outlined in the national security strategy of September 2002.[23] It was based partly on the notion that deterrence and containment might not succeed, and it emphasized the need to resort in appropriate cases to preemptive measures. As President Bush put it, 9/11 made it such that the "doctrine of containment just doesn't hold any water,"[24] that the country could not "wait for the final proof—the smoking gun," which would come in "the form of a mushroom cloud."[25]

Second, Washington was concerned about Iraq's purported ties to terrorism, as reflected in many speeches by top American officials, even if it may have manipulated intelligence on that count. The now-famous Downing Street memo summarizes a July 23, 2002, meeting of British Prime Minister Tony Blair with his top security advisers. In the memo, which is actually the minutes of the meeting, the head of MI6, the British Secret Intelligence Service, reports on his high-level visit to Washington: "Bush wanted to remove Saddam through military action, justified by the conjunction of terrorism and WMD. But the intelligence and facts were being fixed around the policy."[26] Even though the link between al-Qaeda and Iraq was tenuous at best,[27] it was Saddam's misfortune that Iraq represented precisely what the Bush administration feared after 9/11: a dictator with connections to terrorist groups developing WMD. In the words of Defense Secretary Donald Rumsfeld, "we acted because we saw the existing evidence in a new light, through the prism of our experience on September 11," a perspective that reflected the administration's obsession with America's vulnerability to states with WMD and connections to terrorists.[28]

Having been advised in the hours following the attacks on New York and Washington that al-Qaeda was likely responsible, Rumsfeld reportedly asked for existing military plans for an invasion of Iraq; his deputy, Paul Wolfowitz, also pushed for an immediate attack on Iraq, ahead of an invasion of Afghanistan.[29] Meanwhile, President Bush asked for contingency plans to attack Iraq if it were shown that it was involved in the 9/11 attacks or sought to exploit the crisis for its own gain.[30] Like Wolfowitz, Bush made it known early on that he thought Iraq was involved in the 9/11 attacks, and he repeated the mantra that Iraq had had long-standing ties to terrorist groups that were capable and willing to deliver weapons of mass death.[31]

Third, the administration sought to democratize Iraq. On the evening of September 11, 2001, well before the U.S. decision to go to war in Iraq, Bush reassured the nation that the United States "would go forward to defend freedom and all that is good and just in our world."[32] He stressed democratization ahead of the invasion of Iraq,[33] and he continued to repeat it throughout the long war that followed, emphasizing that the United States would support and spread democratic ideas.

## Was the Bush Administration Overconfident?

As suggested earlier in this chapter, determining to what extent the Bush administration was overconfident requires breaking down the case into different dimensions. To what extent did the administration overestimate America's (1) chances of success and (2) capabilities?

### *Overestimating the Chances of Success in Iraq*

The answer to the question about America's prospects for success seems clear. Washington overestimated its prospects for countering the threat of Iraq's WMD and in severing Saddam's connection with al-Qaeda. No WMD were found, nor did it appear that Saddam Hussein had any serious ties to al-Qaeda. The outcome, then, could not be called a success.

Poor information (which I discuss later in this chapter) contributed to overconfidence, but ignoring or not considering information also appeared to result from overconfidence. Richard Haass, who served in the State Department as head of the policy planning staff, described Cheney as too confident that Iraq was close to obtaining nuclear weapons, even though it was not unreasonable to believe at the time that Iran was seeking them.[34] The same was probably true regarding Saddam's alleged connections to terrorism. Cheney either believed that he knew more than the CIA about the supposed connections between Saddam and al-Qaeda, saw the links that he wanted to see or expected to see, or used the purported terror link to push for an invasion that he thought was necessary.[35] It is hard to know which of these motivations was most in play, but we do know that the CIA disagreed with Cheney's position regarding links between Saddam and al-Qaeda.

The administration also overestimated the support that it would receive from global allies. This problem beset the administration from the start, both in the UN, which could not pass a war resolution, and during the war, which lacked a bona fide coalition like the one during the 1990–91 Persian Gulf crisis. The burden of war fell squarely on America's shoulders.

The outcome of the Iraqi invasion was far more disastrous than President Bush and his administration expected.[36] Prior to the invasion and in the early period of the occupation of Iraq, the administration believed that it could achieve success in Iraq in a fairly short period of time, as reflected perhaps in the term "shock and awe," which the Pentagon used to describe the initial military attack on Iraq in 2003. It may have been intended to reflect the overwhelming force that would show Iraqis that Saddam was finished, but it also suggested overconfidence, leading *The Guardian* newspaper to ask if Washington understood how poorly the operation was viewed around the world.[37]

Cheney, like some others in the Bush cabinet, believed that American forces would be "greeted as liberators."[38] Officials simply did not expect the mayhem that resulted. They assumed that Iraq's bureaucracy would remain intact and could run the country and provide Iraqis with basic services. They thought Iraq's armed forces could still provide security after surrendering to U.S. forces and being cleansed of their strongest Baathist elements. With these forces the United States could create a new and effective Iraqi security force. Instead, they would emerge as the vanguard of an insurgency. The initial plan was that the invasion would lead to a speedy handoff of power to Iraqis, but Washington discovered that no durable institutions existed to run a new Iraq.[39] Not only did the United States not anticipate the absence of serious institutions developing, but some in the administration did not understand how ridding the military of Baathist elements would undermine its cohesion and create enemies. As one indication of how the administration was unprepared for reality on the ground, Jay Garner, the head of the civilian Office for Reconstruction and Humanitarian Assistance (discussed below) had planned to stay in Iraq only until June 2003, but his timetable called for a permanent, elected government to be in place by August.[40] The administration was blindsided by postwar problems in Iraq,[41] especially the subsequent massive insurgency. Two months before the invasion, Bush reportedly told Britain's Tony Blair that it was "unlikely there would be internecine warfare between the different religious and ethnic groups.[42]

On May 1, 2003, President Bush landed on the USS *Abraham Lincoln*, which was returning from combat operations in the Persian Gulf, in a fixed-wing aircraft in what some critics called an overly dramatic affair. A few hours later, he gave a speech announcing the end of major combat operations in Iraq. Hanging above him was the warship's banner, which read "Mission Accomplished." In his memoirs, Bush says he noticed the banner and knew it was intended for the returning naval forces, with his speech being about how much work was left to do in Iraq.[43] Bush goes on to say that the media distorted the banner and its message as propaganda that victory was at hand in Iraq, and that is a fair point. The Bush team did not erect the banner. But Bush did state in his speech that the occasion marked the end to major combat operations in Iraq, suggesting that he thought that the serious work that lay ahead had to do with nation building and not dealing with a rising and crippling insurgency. We all now know that the mission was far from accomplished, and in his memoirs Bush describes how much he regretted creating the impression that he thought the mission had been finished.

The affair certainly highlighted a key point that dispels some of the myths about the decision to go to war: it is not that the administration failed to plan for postwar Iraq. The State Department had worked for a year on what was called the "Future of Iraq," a project that clearly reflected the importance of preparing for postwar Iraq. The thousands of pages of reports covered subjects ranging from how to generate and protect oil and agriculture to how to ensure adequate policing in the postwar context. On January 20, 2003, President Bush signed a directive aimed at setting up the Iraq Postwar Planning Office, which would have representatives from ten American federal agencies. Even so, serious blind spots existed. As noted charitably by Douglas Feith, a former Defense Department official in the Bush administration, aspects of postwar planning were put in motion, but "the crippling disorder we call the insurgency was not anticipated with any precision, by either intelligence analysts or policy officials."[44]

We should also consider Colin Powell's claim that Rumsfeld and Bremer did not put into motion the plan that Bush approved. That plan did not call for the army to be totally disbanded and for Baath party members to be fired; rather, it called for a scaled-down, selective version of that approach. President Bush was "surprised" with the outcome, but had to go along with it.[45] In effect, it may well be that Paul Bremer did not execute Bush's wishes, insofar as he understood them, when he decided to formally disband the Iraqi army rather than to vet and retain most of it—and Bush gave him the latitude to do so. Bremer's authority to disband Iraqi forces was so problematic that, according to Michael Gordon and Bernard Trainor, some in the Defense Department saw Bremer as having hijacked the Iraqi mission, expanding its political goals in ways that the president and his cabinet had not anticipated.[46] We might not know the exact dynamics until the proper documents are declassified, but whatever the case, Bush put trust in Bremer to carry out the job and did not stop his actions, making those actions the official position of the United States.

Partly as a result of faulty assumptions about the potential for chaos in Iraq and for a massive insurgency, the administration also believed that it needed fewer troops on the ground than were actually required. As is now well known, Rumsfeld called for small, highly maneuverable forces to conduct military operations in the post–Cold War era. Yet the military largely disagreed that this strategy would work in Iraq. During the planning stages of the war, Army Chief of Staff General Shinseki testified to the U.S. Senate Armed Services Committee that, based on military and other governmental studies, "something in the order of several hundred thousand soldiers" would probably be required for postwar Iraq. His view put him at odds publicly with Rumsfeld and Wolfowitz and diminished his influence.[47] They believed that his figure was far off the mark and that closer to one hundred thousand troops would be needed. Later, after American-led forces ran into significant trouble, President Bush acknowledged that Shinseki was on target, as did the head of U.S. Central Command, John Abizaid.[48] What began as a disaster was possibly turned around because of America's strategy called "the surge," which seemed to vindicate Shinseki. In January 2007, Bush announced a new approach to the war in Iraq at the time when the insurgency appeared to be escalating out of control, and Democrats in Washington were criticizing him for not securing Iraq well enough for American troops to come home. Rather than withdraw, Bush decided to ramp up U.S. efforts. The surge aimed to beef up the U.S. counterinsurgency strategy. To bolster this approach, Bush ordered the deployment of more than twenty thousand soldiers into Iraq and extended the tour of most army troops in country and some of the marines already in Anbar Province. Anbar Province faced the most critical unrest that the Bush administration aimed to quell and reverse so that a unified, self-governing, democratic federal Iraq could emerge. The surge changed the focus for the U.S. military toward helping Iraqis secure key neighborhoods, protect the local population, build their own forces, and achieve reconciliation among political and ethnic factions.[49]

The administration generally misestimated the challenges of rebuilding an entire nation in the heart of the Arab world, where the United States was not well liked and where it would not get much support even from regional allies who saw the democratization drive as a threat to their own autocratic regimes. This should not have come as a great surprise. History was littered with outsiders coming to the Middle East only to be attacked and driven out. The British, of course, had suffered that fate in Iraq earlier in the twentieth century.

Within six months of Bush's "Mission Accomplished" address, over 120,000 American troops were in Iraq facing daily attacks by a resilient and growing insurgency. The story is now familiar. Once the administration realized that a major insurgency was in play, it underestimated its potency. Some of Saddam's former military and intelligence personnel, along with other disaffected Sunnis who had lost power when Saddam fell, became a potent guerrilla force. Meanwhile, al-Qaeda tried to use the chaos as an opportunity to add to the insurgency and to gain recruits among Iraq's citizens, failing miserably in the end partly due to brutal tactics that killed many Iraqis, as well as to successful U.S. military action.

By the time that U.S. forces began their withdrawal from Iraq in 2010, over 4,400 U.S. service personnel were killed and well over thirty thousand had been wounded in action. Hundreds of soldiers from other countries were killed, as well, and many thousands of Iraqis lost their lives. The nonpartisan Congressional Research Service estimates that the United States will have spent more than $800 billion in funding the war by the end of fiscal year 2011.[50] Some argue that this figure will be far higher when we account for the impact of the war on the U.S. budget and economy, the cost of care for wounded soldiers returning home, and in terms of the broader opportunity costs of having spent much money on war that could have been used elsewhere.

The cost of direct U.S. military operations—not including long-term costs such as taking care of wounded veterans—already exceeds the cost of the twelve-year war in Vietnam and is more than double the cost of the Korean War. Nobel Prize winner for economics Joseph Stiglitz as well as Karen Bilmes believe that the Iraq War will eventually cost $3 trillion, which is many times more than the Bush administration estimated. On the eve of war, Larry Lindsey, President Bush's economic adviser and head of the National Economic Council, suggested that costs might reach $200 billion.[51] Three trillion dollars may well be exaggerated, but even if the true cost were $1 trillion, it would still be shockingly large, especially if one takes into account opportunity costs or what the United States could have done with those monies.

In 2010 and 2011, the United States decreased its presence in Iraq in line with President Barack Obama's pledge during the 2008 presidential campaign. What was once a force of over 140,000 troops was trimmed to approximately fifty thousand by September 2010, and most remaining forces were removed by the end of 2011.

One can be confident and still fail miserably, or be overconfident and succeed. Either way, there is value in seeing how goals line up with outcomes. In the Iraq case, knowing that the outcomes were out of line with goals suggests overconfidence, because it highlights how American leaders overestimated their chances of success.

## Overestimating Capabilities?

Did the administration believe that its capabilities were better than they turned out to be? Probably not. It is possible to overestimate the chances of success without overestimating capabilities because many factors aside from capabilities affect the chances of success. The administration's estimations of its own capabilities appear to have been largely on target. Prior to the invasion, it expected that simultaneous air and ground assaults would decapitate Iraq's forces and destroy its command structure quickly, leading to the collapse of the military and the regime. American-led forces accomplished this goal in about three weeks. There were no reports of serious incompetence among the forces.

As suggested above, the postwar planning for some military-related operations was bungled. Perhaps there was no clear guidance from the Pentagon to the military on how to restore order in Baghdad and how to create an interim government.[52] But there is a difference between effective strategy and performance. The military itself, apart from having a dubious strategy, did not appear to perform poorly in trying to stabilize Iraq in the postwar period. One could argue that the administration thought that it could stabilize Iraq with a smaller military force than it really needed. But that's not an overestimation of capability as much as an overestimation of the chances of success in Iraq.

One might argue that Washington overestimated its intelligence capabilities, believing that Iraq had WMD. But it is equally plausible to argue that even enhanced intelligence would have reached similar conclusions about Iraq's WMD. Saddam sought to mislead inspectors about his WMD, and there is no great antidote to strategic deception by a dictator who holds the reins of power and information. It may explain why intelligence services around the world, not just those of the United States, were persuaded that Iraq had WMD. Of course, believing that Saddam was pursuing a WMD program and justifying war are not the same. Even if one believed that he had WMD, one could still argue that it was not worth war.

## Should the Administration Have Known Better?

In assessing overconfidence, we rarely ask if the actor should have known better. There is a danger of saying that overconfidence exists if foreign policy actions fail or run into serious problems. One might argue that the Bush administration could not have known that Iraq would prove so difficult, stressing that it faced obstacles that most people would not have foreseen, even if they were not overconfident, and that hindsight is 20/20. This defense is not without merit, given the great complexity of prediction in world politics, but it still seems weak.

When we tell others that they should have known better, we mean in large part that there was enough information about the costs and benefits of various options to choose a better option. I argue that this was largely the case in Iraq. Why?

It is not clear to what extent studies conducted in various branches of government reached the White House, and if they did reach it, to what extent these studies or broader expert opinion were carefully considered. But it appears that much information did not reach the top. In fact, important studies highlighted the threats of invading and occupying Iraq.[53] Individuals inside and outside of government raised concerns about the challenges of stabilizing Iraq but none of this information influenced the decision-making process, which contributed to a poor policy outcome.[54]

It was almost gospel in academia that stabilizing Iraq would prove quite difficult, a notion that was also considered in the defense and intelligence communities within and outside Washington. At a conference at Joint Forces Command headquarters in Suffolk, Virginia, attendees repeatedly considered that if the United States "breaks Iraq," it will then "own it," with unclear consequences.[55] Such statements commonly referred to the fact that Washington would inherit the troubles generated by its own invasion. It was understood that crushing Saddam would be the easy part, and the rest would be difficult.

Paul Pillar, the national intelligence officer responsible for Middle East affairs from 2002 to 2005, painted an even more damning portrait in an article in *Foreign Affairs* and in a subsequent book.[56] He asserted that the administration shockingly ignored official intelligence reports and even claimed that the first request he received from any superior did not come until one year into the war, despite the fact that he was the person in charge of coordinating all of the intelligence community's assessments regarding Iraq,[57] and that other intelligence officials were similarly ignored.[58]

It might never be fully evident to what extent the administration, or particular members within it, manipulated intelligence to justify war, but a number of thinkers make that case and argue that the administration was misleading to boot.[59] The goal here is not to provide a speculative analysis on that count. It is only important to raise it as one key factor to consider in explaining the American approach toward war.

Two official inquiries by the Senate Intelligence Committee in 2004 and the Robb–Silberman commission in March 2005 found no evidence that political pressure by the Bush administration contributed to these intelligence failures. The inquiries did find that Cheney and others had encouraged analysts to rethink their findings, but even so, it did not lead them to different conclusions. The inquiries did not have access to White House documents, however, and their method of collecting data, according to some high-level officials, was not nuanced enough to understand the administration's true role.[60]

The inquiries also found that political pressure by the administration did not contribute to intelligence failures, but they left open the question of the extent to which the administration exaggerated the threat from Iraq—and al-Qaeda in particular—to justify war.[61] For his part, Pillar claims that the administration manipulated intelligence to justify the decision to invade Iraq, which it had already made in rather quick fashion.[62] Haass recalls that the president instructed counterterrorism coordinator Richard Clarke to look for a connection between Iraq and 9/11 when there was "no reason to suspect one," reflecting a "desire to justify a course of action Bush was already inclined to take."[63]

We can also point out that the 1991 Gulf War could have been partly instructive about the possible effects of invading Iraq. George H. W. Bush and his cabinet didn't want to go into Baghdad after the 1991 Iraq War for various reasons, including the fear of ending up in a quagmire for years.[64] The conditions in 1991 and 2003 were not the same, of course, but it is telling that the United States had been highly cautious of invading Iraq and did not even consider it seriously. Marching on Baghdad at the end of the 1991 war, when U.S.-led forces had already routed the Iraqi military, would have been easier militarily than in 2003, when the efficacy of Iraq's military was less known.

Brent Scowcroft, the national security advisor and close friend to the elder Bush who played a crucial role behind the scenes of the 1990–91 crisis, argued in the *Wall Street Journal* that Iraq should not be invaded. In his view, containment was working quite well, and an invasion would impede the war on terrorism and destabilize the region.[65] This opinion probably also reflected the views of President Bush, given the long-standing friendship between the two men. The president certainly did not come out in favor of invading Iraq.

In any case, the argument against invading Iraq was extremely prominent and could not have been lost on the administration. Coming from such a well-respected, experienced thinker so critical in planning the 1991 Gulf War gave the argument greater credibility. Scowcroft had no ax to grind; he was not a political pundit, and he was not playing party politics. The same can be said of James Baker and Lawrence Eagleburger, the two secretaries of state under the administration of the elder Bush who also issued their own challenges to going to war in Iraq.[66] Both had major experience in U.S. foreign policy in the Middle East.

Prominent American military leaders also argued against the war. For his part, General Wesley Clark, the head of the U.S. NATO force in the Kosovo War, wrote a long piece bemoaning the Bush administration's Iraq plan, as did Norman Schwarzkopf, who led U.S. forces against Iraq in the 1990–91 Gulf War. General Anthony Zinni, Bush's former top envoy to the Middle East, argued that war with Iraq "would stretch U.S. forces too thin and make unwanted enemies in the volatile region," and noted how interesting it was that all the generals were against it while Bush administration, which had never fired a shot, was for it.[67] And Shinseki, as noted earlier, warned that a much larger force was needed to stabilize Iraq, given the magnitude of the task at hand.

For their part, a prominent group of scholars from the realist school of international relations took out a large advertisement in the *New York Times* warning of the dangers of invading Iraq. They emphasized that America could win the war but then could be stuck in Iraq for years trying to rebuild the country.[68]

## The Sources of Overconfidence

There are various explanations of overconfidence from multiple disciplines. Even neuroscience has pitched in to the explanatory game, with some neuroscientists believing that testosterone may play a role. Experimental war games underscore that people are overconfident; that this contributes to war-like behavior, which is more prominent among males than females; and that testosterone plays a role in this process.[69] Others assume that overconfidence arises from various psychological needs, such as self-enhancement.[70] But while biological and psychological explanations are interesting, what can explain overconfidence in the Iraq case, if one accepts that the physiology or behavior of individual actors was in play? While the answer might be more conjecture and academic exercise, some potential reasons can be offered. It is important to understand what drives overconfidence in foreign policy in order to avoid similar errors in the future.

### Information Problems

It will take years to determine what mix of bad information, neglected information, and manipulated information affected decision making leading up to the invasion of Iraq. I don't intend to differentiate between these "information problems," as I refer to them here. However, problems with information certainly played a role—not only in the belief that Iraq had WMD, but also in misestimating the chances of success in Iraq—which created a specter of a much greater Iraqi threat than existed, facilitated the administration's efforts to gain domestic support for war, and predisposed key officials to believe that Iraq could be refashioned without great trouble.

In its defense, the administration insisted that it had made a sound decision based on the evidence at hand, faulty as it was, and challenged criticism that it had cooked the books for war. Reflecting the administration's position, Powell was "disappointed" that the intelligence was not on target but claimed the administration had not misled the world and the American people, because government officials had believed what they said about Iraq. "We thought Iraq had stockpiles of WMD."[71]

Prior to leaving the White House, President Bush admitted that the decision to go to war against Saddam Hussein was based on flawed intelligence, and that this intelligence mishap was the biggest regret of his presidency. He still supported the decision to go to war and to get rid of Saddam Hussein. Later, in his 2010 book *Decision Points*, he said that the failure to find WMD was a failure of information.[72]

## An Ineffective Media

We usually think of the media as watchdogs over government, tasked with uncovering misdeeds and ineffective management and with questioning politicians. Yet qualitative and quantitative study finds that the media were weak in questioning the march to war. In 2003, a study released by Fairness and Accuracy in Reporting found that the network news disproportionately focused on pro-war sources. According to the study, sixty-four percent of all sources were in favor of the Iraq War, while total anti-war sources made up ten percent of the media (only three percent of U.S. sources were anti-war). The study stated that "viewers were more than six times as likely to see a pro-war source as one who was anti-war; with U.S. guests alone, the ratio increases to 25 to 1."[73] At the qualitative level, *Feet to the Fire*, by Kristina Borjesson, found that pre–Iraq War news coverage was shoddy, and in it she interviewed top journalists to try to understand why.[74]

Political scientist Chaim Kaufman argues that the administration had decided to invade Iraq and then fixed the intelligence around this goal, manipulating and distorting it to support foregone conclusions. In his view, one reason they could get away with it is that the media and institutions did not play their proper roles.[75] Had the media been more intrusive and doggedly questioned the administration's policy, overconfidence might have been tempered, even if officials believed that Saddam had to go no matter what. They still would have faced greater media pressure, which might have translated into more pressure from the public and Congress, as well as more internal debates about the dangers of invading Iraq. Even if such pressures did not deter an invasion, they might have forced greater consideration for how to conduct affairs in post-Saddam Iraq.

## The Cold War Is Over

If it is true that the Bush team saw the world predominantly in terms of the U.S.–Soviet rivalry during the Cold War, then it is possible that it saw the fall of the Soviet Union as a grand sign of American preeminence in world politics. With this struggle over, the Bush team may have seen Iraq as theirs to conquer and to transform, with history's tailwind behind them and the world's most powerful military at their disposal. Moscow was no longer aligned with Iraq, as it had been in the Cold War, and it was unable to check American prowess. Meanwhile, the idea that American capitalism and democracy beat out communism might have been added impetus to export democracy to Iraq. This combination of developments and American perceptions may well have contributed to overconfidence in the Iraq case.

## Analogies Misplaced

As I have argued elsewhere, the Bush administration could have seen America's previous successes in Iraq in 1991 as reason to think it could win in 2003. After all, after some serious aerial bombardment, Saddam's million-man army folded quickly in a one-hundred-hour ground war, despite his calls for a bloody "mother of all battles." The victory was so lopsided that Washington could have marched on Baghdad and taken it without much initial opposition.

George W. Bush may have learned from his father's experience that attacking Iraq can succeed, but that allowing Saddam to stay in power can prove quite troublesome. Perhaps he wanted to finish the job that his father had started. As Richard Haass put it, Bush "may have sought to accomplish what his father did not."[76] But the 1991 analogy was prominent not just in the president's mind but in the minds of top decision makers, and in a way that is somewhat unique in presidential history. Bush's administration included key members of his father's team, all of whom had been involved in the Gulf War. Defense Secretary Dick Cheney became the powerful vice president, and Colin Powell, who had been chairman of the Joint Chiefs of Staff, became secretary of state. Cheney's prominent aide Paul Wolfowitz became deputy secretary of defense. Richard Haass, who had been the top National Security Council analyst on the Middle East, became director of policy planning at the State Department. Not all favored war, but certainly Cheney and Wolfowitz supported it. And while Rumsfeld was not in the elder Bush's cabinet, he and others had lived through the 1990–91 crisis and Saddam's subsequent challenges to America and its allies. In fact, the analogy might have worked at multiple levels, such as in suggesting to them the example of the elder Bush's strong determination against Saddam Hussein—something that may have worked on their own thinking in conscious or subconscious ways.

The cognitive bias of analogical thinking could have played a role insofar as decision makers analogized back to the 1991 Gulf victory, and from that experience assumed that victory was possible once again, while the more abstract warnings about what might happen in an invasion of Iraq did not gain cognitive traction. Perhaps it is easier to reflect analogically on past events than to think rationally about things that did not occur. Moreover, as Thomas Pickering argues, victories in places like Bosnia and Afghanistan against the Taliban following the

9/11 terrorist attacks may have contributed to overconfidence. In this sense, analogies to past wars could have influenced the decision to go to war with Iraq, even though the case of Iraq in 2003 was quite different. If true, it would be a good example of one cognitive bias working together with and worsening another. The analogical bias reinforced the overconfidence bias to make for decision making that did not foresee significant problems.

### President George W. Bush's Personality and Decision-Making Style

Several aspects of President Bush's style were salient. He prided himself on being the decider, on making tough decisions based on principle and sticking to them. This personality trait can be connected to overconfidence, because at the very least it does not produce great caution and dissembling, which could prevent someone from becoming overconfident.

Along these lines, President Bush may have also sought to set his own independent course as a determined leader rather than as a reputed follower of others. This motivation may have been reinforced by widespread criticism that Cheney, one of his father's closest advisers, actually ran the administration. Such criticism could not have been lost on Bush and certainly not on his advisers, who may have regarded the Iraq War as an opportunity to establish the president's credentials as a strong leader. Interestingly, when asked by reporter Bob Woodward whether he had consulted with his father before making the decision to invade Iraq, President Bush asserted that "there is a higher Father that I appeal to," which seemed to diminish his father's role.

Bush appeared to make the final war decision outside any committee or group. Numerous accounts support the notion, as put forth by Richard Haass, that "there was no meeting or set of meetings at which the pros and cons were debated and a formal decision taken."[77] Powell recalled there was not a "moment when we all made our recommendations and [Bush] made a decision."[78] Rumsfeld apparently could not recall if there ever was a "formal moment" when the President asked him if America should go to war.[79] Tenet also observes that meetings focused not on whether to go to war but on what actions would be required to support war, if the United Stated decided to go to war.[80] Reporters who interviewed Bush administration officials across departments and agencies reached a similar conclusion, that the decision to invade, as Rice is quoted as saying, occurred without a "decision meeting."[81]

These insider views sketch a portrait of a president who, perhaps in close interaction with Cheney and a few other advisers, made a war decision well ahead of his advisers and of any formal decision-making discussions. This then set the agenda for how to achieve this goal—an agenda that was pursued in numerous high-level meetings among his principals and their deputies. Bush may well have canvassed some of his leading advisers in a way that allowed him to make his decision to invade Iraq, but his decision-making style, as some have observed, might not have been well organized.[82]

In addition to having a penchant toward being the decider, Bush had vision. Whereas President George H. W. Bush had been repeatedly criticized for lacking vision, his son exemplified a worldview—whatever one thinks of its merits—in the post-9/11 period. Although his vision may have come from the gut, it adhered to a unilinear view of history. In contrast to a cyclical view of history, where the afflictions of international relations repeat over time, President George W. Bush held a firm belief in human progress—in this case, the democratization of a challenging region. The vision of democratizing the Middle East, like other grand visions, could have fed overconfidence. Throughout history, ideologues have tended to see what is possible and to downplay obstacles. They are driven by and toward their vision, making other considerations less important.

President George W. Bush was also far more tied to religious interpretations than his father. In his speeches he raised—significantly more often than most presidents—the issue of religion and his relationship with God. From his assertion on September 12, 2001, that he was in the "Lord's hands,"[83] to his rhetoric about the forces of good and evil, to his reference to the War on Terror as a crusade,[84] Bush was prone to make religious interpretations of events.[85] It should be said that his notion of crusade was different from that of most Muslims:[86] He saw it as an effort to confront evil terrorists and those who supported them, whereas Muslims tended to interpret the term through the lens of their difficult historical experiences with the brutal Christian crusades.

In the spring of 2004, Bush referred several times to his belief that a higher power was guiding his actions. The United States had historically promoted the liberal tradition as a transnational set of ideas and largely kept religion and politics separate. In keeping religion out of politics, the United States differed fundamentally from Islamist states. Although President Bush was not deviating from that tradition (nor did he speak for all Americans or administration officials), his words were enough to raise questions in the Muslim world about a Judeo–Christian showdown with Islam.

One might expect that Bush would be heavily criticized for his copious religious references, and to some extent he was. Yet even during the presidential election, the campaign of Senator John Kerry avoided openly criticizing Bush's religious tone. Bush may have seen Iraq partly through the prism of religion. The United States was a God-fearing Christian nation, and Iraq was fit for transformation—an impulse that meshed well with his brand of American exceptionalism and with his visions of a democratized Iraq and Middle East.

## Overoptimism

Overoptimism describes the human tendency to believe that things are more likely to turn out well than poorly. The optimism bias causes individuals to believe that they have less risk than others of experiencing a negative event, such as being a victim of crime, or that they are more likely than others to experience a positive event, such as winning at gambling. Stock market traders may think that they are less exposed to the risk of losses, and people in general may be sanguine about the outcome of planned actions. [87] Most people believe that they are more likely than average to live past eighty.[88] If you ask a room full of students who thinks they will finish in the top fifty percent of the class, around eighty percent of them on average will respond in the affirmative.[89] In addition, students typically believe they can complete assignments far faster than they can.[90] All are examples of wishful thinking.

Although the optimism bias applies to both positive and negative events, research suggests that the bias is stronger for negative events. And it can fuel other biases, such as overconfidence and the planning fallacy. In the 2003 Iraq War, leaders did not appear to consider the possibility that their policies would go awry despite the high chances for a negative outcome. Their optimism in turn contributed to overconfidence, or to the belief that the accuracy of one's judgments is much better than objective accuracy would suggest.

## Conclusion

The United States was dealt a blow on September 11, 2001, by a criminal terrorist group. In response, it invaded Afghanistan and Iraq. This chapter is not a critique of whether the invasion of Iraq made sense. But the evidence suggests that American decision makers were overconfident in deciding to invade and failed to recognize the inherent difficulty of stabilizing and rebuilding Iraq. It is always easy to criticize in hindsight, but the Bush administration probably should have expected greater problems in invading Iraq.

Still, a number of qualifications are in order. First, when arguing that an administration or president was overconfident, we should not confuse overconfidence with efforts to garner support or to appear strong in front of the public, allies, and foreign enemies. Such political goals may have added to what appeared outwardly to be overconfidence. Second, we must be careful not to engage in backward flow, where we see that a foreign policy action produces failure or aspects of failure and then assume that overconfidence existed. Examining whether an actor should have known better helps avoid this trap. Third, it is important not to overemphasize the role of overconfidence, as other factors are always in play in explaining decisions and outcomes. Overconfidence may have contributed to the American decision to go to war, for instance, but so did a range of other noncognitive factors. In fact, these factors were much more important in this case, including concern about WMD and Saddam Hussein's potential hegemony in the region. The rational actor model would highlight those factors by stressing threats to U.S. national interests, suggesting the need to look beyond just one decision-making model and to integrate insights derived from multiple models. I created a framework for doing so in my book *Explaining Foreign Policy*, which applied what I called an integrated approach for explaining foreign policy in general.[91]

Finally, we should be careful about making sweeping conclusions regarding the negative impact of overconfidence. Sometimes overconfidence produces positive results. As Dan Ariely notes, neuroscience has shown that emotions are usually needed to drive people to act. Optimism can drive overconfidence, pushing us to take positive steps like going back to school or starting a business. Maybe certain types of optimism or optimism at certain times (e.g., recession, crises) produce an overall good for society, even if it leads to the downfall of particular individuals. If so, it would be interesting to better understand when optimism is beneficial and what pushes it to become overoptimism.[92]

While this work cautions against being overconfident, can overconfidence be avoided? It's not so simple. To start, one might not be aware of their overconfidence. And even if one is aware, it's sometimes hard to distinguish confidence, a positive trait, from overconfidence. But being more aware of how one thinks could help. For policy makers or laypeople, awareness can follow from consciously and carefully considering the costs and benefits of options and all reasonable inputs and information, which should yield a good sense of the capabilities at hand and the chances for success.

# CHAPTER FIVE

# U.S. Energy Policy

## Short-Term Bias

Why hasn't the United States developed a comprehensive energy policy to decrease its significant consumption of oil, which amounts to one-fourth of the
roughly eighty-five to ninety million barrels of oil that the world consumes each
day? This question is especially salient today, as we understand better that dependence on oil affects U.S. foreign policy and the stability of the entire American
economy.[1] Energy security is increasingly linked to major economic, security,
and environmental problems, including war, terrorism, national rivalries, and
climate change.[2]

Oil plays a central role in the stories told in this book. Coming full circle, Washington was concerned when Moscow invaded Afghanistan in 1979 that it might
threaten the oil-rich Persian Gulf. The Afghanistan invasion was not unimportant but could not have motivated massive American countermeasures without
the threat it posed to the Gulf. Meanwhile, the Iran-Contra affair, while driven by
concern for the hostages, was also motivated by the desires to gain more influence in the region and to enhance relations with Iran—which would have been
far less important were it not for oil in the Persian Gulf. In this mix of ongoing
events, al-Qaeda emerged and developed. Al-Qaeda was not only empowered by
the Afghanistan experience and fueled by oil monies, but was motivated to attack
the United States on September 11 in part because of America's thirst for oil, as
seen through its distorted religious lens, including the U.S. response to Iraq's
invasion of Kuwait. The streams in history released by all of these events contributed to the U.S.-led invasion of Iraq in 2003—a war that was not about oil but
one that probably could not have occurred if not for these preceding oil-related
events.

Against this backdrop, it is appropriate to look at America's energy policy.
In the absence of a serious and comprehensive policy, America's dependence

on foreign oil, and its attendant threats to national security, has become more important than ever.

## Argument: Shortsightedness Can Lead to Long-Term Problems

Plenty of reasons have been offered for America's lack of a comprehensive energy policy. In part, efforts to produce sensible plans have failed because the energy and automobile industries, which depend on high consumption of oil and other natural resources, used policy pressures to influence the public, Congress, and the executive branch.[3] Other reasons may be that members of Congress support American energy firms to protect jobs in their districts; that American bureaucracies are too inefficient to address the problem; and that oil is so cheap that other alternatives make less sense, meaning they are not pursued or rejected by the marketplace. There's truth in all these arguments and they explain a good part of the picture.

But we hear far less about cognitive biases and how they work. Short-term thinking is not just a tendency—it can be a psychological proclivity. I argue that thinking in the short term has contributed significantly to the oil dependence problem, partly because political leaders operate with elections in mind, and partly because voters tend to support politicians who offer the best handouts in the near future despite possible longer-term consequences. Consumers often focus on short-run gratification, predisposing them against actions that can decrease oil dependence such as higher gas taxes or buying more efficient, higher-cost vehicles.

To what extent is short-term thinking irrational? Irrational for whom? And over what period of time? For example, polluting or wasting energy might seem rational to an individual if it represents the best cost–benefit option, while rejecting efforts to decrease oil dependence can be rational for a politician up for re-election. But whether such actions make sense in the short term for the consumer or politician, they are not rational for the nation as a whole over time if they prevent informed consideration of options for enhancing national welfare.

Americans leaders have occasionally displayed long-term thinking during times of crisis, but these responses were usually short lived. Short-term thinking might explain this tendency, but so can cognitive biases embedded in a famous theory of decision making, otherwise known as prospect theory, which I examine at the end of this chapter.

## America's Energy Record

When we think of American dependence on oil, we usually mean two things: dependence on foreign oil and the country's overall oil consumption, including what we produce at home. The first measures the amount of net imports (our imports minus our exports of oil) as part of our overall consumption of oil, while the latter measures our overall consumption of foreign and domestic oil. Some strides have been made in decreasing dependence on foreign oil, although only in the post-2008 period and not really as a result of U.S. energy policy. Until then, the record was outright sketchy even in reducing dependence on foreign oil.

### Decreasing Foreign Oil Dependence: Making Progress but Not Enough

Virtually every American president in recent memory has called for a major project to reduce American oil dependence. On November 7, 1973, Richard Nixon called for proposals to deal with the energy crisis caused by the Arab oil embargo and for a national undertaking that "by the end of the decade" would allow the United States to "have developed the potential to meet our own energy needs without depending on any foreign energy source."[4] Gerald Ford followed, calling in January 1975 for a grand, ten-year plan to decrease oil dependence. Jimmy Carter famously called oil dependence one of the greatest threats to American security, asserting that his energy program was the "moral equivalent of war."[5] Most subsequent presidents have echoed these ambitions. Bill Clinton in 2000 said that "we need a long-term energy strategy to maximize conservation and the development of alternative sources of energy."[6]

The United States cut its oil imports by half after the 1973 Arab oil embargo between 1977 and 1982, representing an important advance in decreasing oil dependence.[7] But America's victory was short lived. As memories of the oil shock faded, so did America's commitment to longer-run energy measures. Since the mid-1980s, the United States has increasingly imported the amount of oil it consumes. The share of foreign oil consumed by America has grown from thirty-five percent in 1973 to around sixty percent in the twenty-first century,[8] despite promises and efforts to decrease foreign oil dependence during that period. By 2013, the share was down to about forty-two percent.

The significant drop in oil dependence from 2005 to 2012 was partly due to the U.S. boom in oil production—one that many people see as a game-changing, tectonic shift in our energy picture. The U.S. oil industry now produces 1.6 million more barrels of oil each day than it did in 2008. That's a significant increase in a world that consumes around eighty-nine million barrels per day, with the United States accounting for about a quarter of that amount. This energy boom is resulting partly from the use of two key technologies that allow for the reclamation of "tight oil" and natural gas. In thinking about oil and gas drilling, we might imagine lakes of oil underground that drillers exploit. That's not the case at all with shale oil. Shale oil exists in what appears to be solid rock. We might see little or no oil in these areas, but in others it would be more apparent. In most cases, only high-tech machinery can actually detect the oil, which is stuck between the grains of porous rock like sandstone, or at best resides in small oil reservoirs that are hidden otherwise.

The first technology to exploit this rock is called hydraulic fracturing. It shoots pressurized liquids into compact, underground rock formations and loosens up the energy, so to speak. The second technology is horizontal drilling. Horizontal drilling provides access to these oil and gas reservoirs from top to bottom. Drillers can drill them from the side, where more reservoir rock is exposed, providing much better results with far fewer drilling wells and attempts.

## Decreasing Overall Oil Dependence

While some progress has been made in decreasing dependence on foreign oil, that progress has been made mainly by private firms on private lands, and not because of new U.S. energy policy; meanwhile, there has been little progress in reducing oil consumption in the United States. As of 2012, we still use about as much oil as we did one decade ago, notwithstanding the financial crisis of 2008 and its aftermath, which suppressed oil consumption, and we now use much more oil than in past decades. And that's not likely to change soon.

Presidents have often blamed the opposing political party for not addressing oil dependence. Bemoaning the lack of a comprehensive energy policy, President George W. Bush asserted how unfortunate it was that "Democrats in Congress are standing in the way of further development."[9] For his part, President Barack Obama claimed that energy policy was hostage to "the same political gridlock, the same inertia that has held us back for decades."[10] While on the campaign trail in his bid for the presidency, Obama often repeated a similar tune: "For our economy, our security, and the future of our planet, I will set a clear goal as president: in ten years, we will finally end our dependence on oil from the Middle East. Washington's been talking about our oil addiction for the last thirty years, and McCain has been there for twenty-six of them . . . Now is the time to end this addiction, and to understand that drilling is a stop-gap measure, not a long-term solution."[11]

The Obama administration significantly elevated the focus on overall oil dependence. On March 31, 2010, at Andrews Air Force Base, Obama announced a "comprehensive plan for energy security," stating that "moving towards clean energy is about our security. It's also about our economy. And it's about the future of our planet." In a major speech in March 2011, he called for a one-third cut in oil imports by 2025. Citing a plethora of problems associated with oil dependence that echoed statements made by Jimmy Carter in the 1970s, Obama said that we have delayed too long in dealing with oil dependence. "We've been down this road before," he said, acknowledging that several past presidents have made similar calls for greater energy independence. But, he added, "we can't rush to action when gas prices are high and then hit the snooze button when prices are low again."[12]

To be sure, under President George W. Bush, but especially under Obama, the United States made strides in trying to decrease oil dependence. In the post-9/11 environment, and with American troops in both Iraq and Afghanistan, the connection between oil and security grew stronger in the public mind. The 2005 Energy Policy Act was the first major energy-related legislation of any kind since the early 1990s, and the even more far-reaching Energy Independence and Security Act of 2007 soon followed. While lacking in some ways, these acts sought to decrease oil dependence in general and dependence on oil imports in particular.[13] The 2005 act contained tax credits for the purchase of hybrid vehicles, while the 2007 act raised fuel economy standards, and both acts mandated greater use of alternative transportation fuels.

It is important not just to decrease American oil dependence by producing more oil at home, but also to decrease overall oil consumption. Why?

Studies by the U.S. Department of Energy show that the direct economic costs of American oil dependence have risen significantly over the past several decades.[14] And Americans are aware of the impact of oil prices. In late 2000, the cost of a barrel of oil reached $30 for the first time since the 1991 Gulf War and for only the second time since the price collapse of the mid-1980s. Then, after dropping briefly during the following two years, the price of oil began a more or less steady rise that ultimately led to a record high of nearly $150 per barrel in mid-2008, before dropping sharply again.

Will America's energy boom deliver lower oil prices, which is what most Americans want and might expect? A recent report by the International Energy Agency concluded that the United States will displace Saudi Arabia—even if temporarily—as the world's largest oil producer by 2020. Current U.S. oil imports of nine to ten million barrels per day are projected to fall to around four million barrels per day within one decade, thanks to technological advances in fracking and horizontal drilling that allow for greater access to otherwise trapped oil and natural gas.

America's energy boom may deliver lower oil prices under some conditions, but not as low as those looking for a short-term fix to U.S. energy problems might think. First, the boom would mean far more if America alone used its own oil resources. But oil is a global commodity. No matter where the oil comes from, buyers will pay roughly the same price for it. And all of America's extra oil will be sold chiefly on global oil markets, not set aside for Americans. As an extreme example, Norway is a net exporter of oil but its citizens pay higher gas prices, even after accounting for its higher fuel taxes.

Second, because oil is traded globally, a supply disruption anywhere in the world affects oil prices for all consumers. Even if the United States were to import little oil because of a homegrown energy boom, Americans would still be vulnerable to global events that raise the price of oil. After all, they can't control instability in Saudi Arabia, attacks on oil facilities in Nigeria, or a plethora of other threats to the flow of oil that would push oil prices higher.

Third, the energy boom probably won't stop oil speculation or the purchase of oil futures for profit rather than to obtain oil. Tens of billions of dollars went into the nation's energy commodity markets in the past few years, earmarked for futures contracts. Institutional and hedge funds are increasingly investing in oil, which has prompted President Obama and others to call for curbs on oil speculation. Data released in March 2011 by Bart Chilton, a member of the Commodity Futures Trading Commission who has urged limits on speculation, suggest that speculators increased their positions in energy markets by sixty-four percent between June 2008 and January 2011. The rub is that, despite the domestic oil boom, speculators will still buy oil futures whenever they think oil prices will rise. Of course, extra American oil on the market might temper speculation under some conditions, but then again, it might not.

Fourth, the Organization of the Petroleum Exporting Countries (OPEC) will not sit by idly if America's boom begins to substantially decrease oil prices. Its members will most likely agree to lower their production to try to keep prices higher. In June 2012, when the price of oil dropped to around $80 a barrel from $107 in March, fellow OPEC producers pressured Saudi Arabia to cut output. Producers need oil revenues to maintain their cradle-to-grave welfare states; otherwise, they could face Arab Spring–type revolts at home, which most oil-rich countries have avoided by using their wealth to quell dissent and to maintain domestic control.

Fifth, a backlash against hydraulic fracturing, which possibly pollutes water supplies, could grow if it is proven to be an environmental hazard. Technological breakthroughs may make fracking safer, but it's not apparent when or if they could be implemented at reasonable cost.

To be sure, the American oil boom has its positives. The world needs all forms of energy to meet rising demand. It could also dampen the impact of oil disruptions, especially if the drilling revolution expands to other countries in the future. America's abundant natural gas can also offset reliance on coal, which is a dirtier energy source. But let's not exaggerate what the energy boom can do for American consumers. At its current pace, the oil boom probably won't significantly lower prices—though it may temper their rise at times. Greater oil independence does not equal greater oil price independence, a fact that is often lost in our national debate.

Likewise, a boom in fossil fuels will not address the problem of climate change; in fact, it might worsen it by diverting our attention from sustainable energies. Decreasing overall oil dependence, partly through sustainable energy practices, remains an important and only partially met goal. It would help protect future generations from climate havoc and wean us from our dependence on the vagaries of oil prices—something critical to a comprehensive energy policy.

## Short-Term Thinking: A Cognitive Bias in Play

In his farewell address, President Dwight Eisenhower told Americans to "avoid the impulse to live only for today, plundering, for our own ease and convenience, the precious resources of tomorrow. We cannot mortgage the material assets of our grandchildren without risking the loss also of their political and spiritual heritage."[15] Although Eisenhower had great experience and insight, he was not the only president to warn of short-term thinking. Many presidents have warned against shortsightedness, and some have tried to address it within the difficult constraints under which they have worked.

Short-term thinking privileges short-term considerations over longer-term ones, although the two interact in complex ways.[16] It's not a revelation to say that individuals often ignore or fail to consider the long-run implications of their actions. That's why they buy clothes and homes that they can't afford. Perhaps they are impulsive. Maybe the future is too murky for them to see. It could be that they need cheering up, or that they simply don't consider what their present actions mean for the future. Perhaps, as Joel Heinin and Roberta Low suggest, the short-term bias has evolutionary origins in that it was advantageous to emphasize short-run benefits and punishments rather than long-term ones in order to enhance reproductive chances.[17]

Whatever the exact cause, a large literature now exists on the conflict people face between seeking immediate pleasure and what is best in the longer term.[18] Studies have demonstrated that people favor rewards received sooner rather than later, although their preferences differ in situations when they must choose between smaller, immediate rewards and larger, delayed ones.[19] Neuroscientists have recently uncovered that stock market investors are hardwired for the short term. They are enticed by short-term gains, which appear to stimulate the emotional centers of the brain, making them feel confident and generally good about themselves.[20] The economic meltdown of 2008 may have been related to the pursuit of immediate rewards, whether by lenders trying to reap profits from questionable loans or homeowners buying property beyond their means.

Behavioral economist David Laibson has presented, in contrast to what classical economic theory predicts, research (including information from brain scans) that shows there's a conflict between short- and longer-term thinking. Laibson, like other scholars,[21] believes that the brain is in conflict. What is called the mesolimbic dopamine reward system—the part of the brain that focuses on rewards—is concrete and immediate. By contrast, the prefrontal cortex sees tomorrow essentially the same as it sees today, and warns of the longer-run effects of today's behavior. It puts a lot of weight on the present, but little on the future.[22] Other scholars have found that the capacity to take into account the long-term effects of our behavior is affected by our prefrontal cortex.[23] Patients with damage to prefrontal regions tend to ignore the consequences of their behavior.[24] The extent of short-term thinking may well depend on a number of factors. In negative emotional states involving threats, for instance, people focus on the short-term, regardless of possible long-term consequences.[25]

The tendency to privilege the short term may extend to decision making in international relations. There is no good reason to believe that short-term thinking displayed in experiments suddenly disappears in the realm of foreign policy. As political scientists Alex Mintz and Karl DeRouen point out, "leaders typically focus on short-term benefits rather than longer-term problems."[26]

## American Energy Policy: Déjà Vu

Decreasing oil dependence is a critical goal for the United States and other countries in the twenty-first century, but Washington needs an appropriate strategy to ensure that energy independence can be achieved. I argue that the central focus needs to be on transportation. Nearly seventy percent of all U.S. oil consumption is attributable to the transportation of people and products. Based on U.S. Department of Transportation statistics, there are over 247.4 million registered vehicles on U.S. roads. Of these, ninety-four percent are two-axle vehicles (e.g., motorcycle, passenger car, light truck, sport utility vehicle, van) owned and operated by individuals for the purposes of personal or family travel.[27] Privately owned vehicles consume the largest portion of America's oil. Analysis of the fleet reveals that the average passenger car in the United States has a fuel efficiency of about 22.1 miles per gallon (mpg), consuming approximately 567 gallons of refined motor fuel per year. The average SUV has a fuel efficiency of about 17.7 mpg, consuming approximately 617 gallons of fuel per year.[28]

The following sections examine what I believe to be the most important approaches for decreasing oil dependence, especially in the transportation sector, and explore the extent of short-term thinking in each: gasoline taxes, Corporate Average Fuel Economy (CAFE) standards, vehicle efficiency, speed limits, and high-speed rail.

Since 2009, legislative energy policy efforts have focused on the creation of a cap-and-trade system for carbon emissions. Although cap and trade might help to limit climate change, it's not focused on decreasing oil dependence and is not discussed in this chapter. Indeed, the bill passed by the House of Representatives in 2009 contained no provisions explicitly aimed at reducing oil consumption. This chapter also doesn't examine biofuels because they have posed an oil alternative only recently, although biofuels have made some strides. For instance, the 2005 Energy Policy Act and the Energy Independence and Security Act of 2007 mandated greater use of biofuels. The 2005 act mandated the production of an increasing amount of ethanol, which has fallen out of favor because it drives up food prices throughout the world, with a disproportionately negative impact on the poor. Meanwhile, the 2007 act ambitiously requires the inclusion of at least thirty-six billion gallons of ethanol and other biofuels in the fuel supply by 2022.

This study also doesn't examine solar, coal, hydropower, nuclear, natural gas, and other forms of energy that produce electricity. We cannot currently use them to decrease oil dependence by much, because increased electricity use does little to decrease gas use, unless we get millions upon millions of electric cars on the road.

### Raising the Gasoline Tax

I argue that opposition to gas taxes results from various factors, including a short-term bias in U.S. energy policy. Despite discussion on increasing America's gas tax following the Arab oil embargo, little was done, in contrast to the much higher tax rates imposed in Japan and the Western European states.[29] The first federal gasoline tax was adopted in 1932 at a level of one cent per gallon, and the tax has increased in small amounts over the past seventy-five years. In 1951, it was raised by two cents per gallon to increase funds for the Korean War. It doubled in 1959, to four cents per gallon, to help fund the construction of the new interstate highway system, and was raised another nine cents per gallon in 1981. Subsequent increases in 1990 and 1993 resulted in our current federal gasoline tax of 18.4 cents per gallon.

Interestingly, according to a study in the *Journal of Economic Literature,* only one group strongly supports gas taxes, and they are not affected by short-term thinking: economists. They include Republicans such as Martin Feldstein, who served as chairman of the Council of Economic Advisers and as chief economic advisor to President Ronald Reagan; Alan Greenspan, who would like to see higher gasoline taxes to increase national security; and N. Gregory Mankiw, chairman of George W. Bush's Council of Economic Advisors. They also include prominent public intellectuals such as Steven Levitt, author of *Freakonomics,* and Nobel laureate and *New York Times* columnist Paul Krugman.

Even General Motors CEO Dan Akerson, who is a Republican, reportedly would like to see the federal gasoline tax boosted by as much as $1 per gallon in order to encourage drivers to choose more fuel-efficient vehicles.[30] If one considers that a gas tax could decrease carbon emissions, reduce dependency on oil, help the environment, and decrease the federal deficit, it could be viewed, as Mankiw put it, as "the closest thing to a free lunch that economics has to offer."[31]

Increasing gas taxes doesn't have to mean increasing the overall tax burden. How? Taxes can be fully or partly "revenue neutral," or offset by other tax cuts; in the payroll tax, for instance. That's not an overall tax increase, though individual states might want to tax gas for revenue generation, as well. Rather, we could increase taxes on gas and decrease them on the payroll, leaving people with no net increase in taxes. In either case, many economists support a gas tax because they understand the value of longer-run market signals. For starters, high oil prices spur efficiency. The 1973 Arab oil embargo made America more able to use oil efficiently for productivity (a notion called energy intensity).

High energy prices also make consumers more likely to purchase fuel-efficient vehicles. High prices for fossil fuels—coal, oil, natural gas—help spur development of alternative energy resources, as solar, wind, and geothermal power generation become cost competitive with traditional fossil fuel–fired power plants. The higher energy prices go, the more entrepreneurs around the world will embrace alternatives.

Scientists agree that the combustion of fossil fuels causes climate change, even though only fifty-two percent of Americans in a March 2012 Gallup Poll agreed. The poll was consistent with views since 2009, but lower than in prior years going back one decade, when as many as sixty-one percent believed global warming was already a major problem.[32] To head off disaster, climate experts say we need to slash our greenhouse gas emissions sharply—as much as eighty to ninety percent—by 2050, which would immediately result in reductions of about twenty percent per decade (two percent per year). Advanced technologies must be part of meeting that challenge, and high energy prices are the fastest way to spur those along. Despite the fact that many economists argue that higher fuel taxes would be the most efficient way to reduce oil consumption, little has been done. Virtually every sector of American society is against increased gas taxes.

Politicians often see raising taxes as political suicide. For them, it may not be worth pursuing even a small tax increase because of the relatively small benefits and the large political opposition. Kristin Sipes and Robert Mendelsohn point to the significant opposition to a modest five-cent increase proposed by the Clinton administration as an example.[33] Politicians may ignore proposals that involve an immediate, painful cost even if they provide long-term benefits. The short-term costs can hurt them politically, while the abstract, longer-run benefits cannot help them that much. Our election cycle promotes short-term gratification. The term of the lower house of Congress is a mere two years, so that election time is always on the minds of elected officials, focusing greater attention on short-term approaches to major issues, especially if the longer-term implications are hard to explain, may disturb voters, or could cut campaign funding.

Taking action on oil dependence often falls into this category. High oil prices represent an immediate threat that voters want addressed, but trying to address them in the short run sometimes undermines longer-run thinking. As the former director of the U.S. Energy Information Administration from 1993 to 2000, Jay Hakes learned first hand the challenges of decreasing oil dependence. He stresses that success requires a longer-term approach, against the grain of political motivations. Hakes points out what he considers typical by referring to Vice President Walter Mondale's description of decision making: "In the Carter administration, we talked about the short-term pain and the long-term gain, and boy did we emphasize that short-term pain."[34] And his administration privileged longer-term thinking on oil dependence more than other administrations. In sharp contrast, European gasoline prices are roughly double what they are here in the United States. European economies are also much more energy efficient than ours, even though they also face short-term challenges. As Chancellor of the Exchequer Vince Cable noted in June 2009, "long-term thinking is difficult in the current political crisis, when most politicians are obsessed by tomorrow's headlines . . . but our future as a country depends much more on our ability to plan ahead for the next oil shock and the post-oil world."[35]

Voters are focused on the short term and politicians know it. Polls of the

American public repeatedly show that sixty to seventy percent are against even modestly raising the gas tax.[36] And surveys show that they especially hate high gas prices. Many politicians and citizens argue that higher gas taxes would hurt the economy by taking money out of the pockets of citizens and raising transportation costs, and they would not consider that to be a short-term problem. Others argue that we are sacrificing longer-run goals such as energy independence and are staving off the harmful impact of fossil fuels on the environment, which would produce even in economic terms much better long-term gains than anything we can save in the short run. As evidence mounts on the costs of using fossil fuels, the latter case becomes more plausible.

In any event, a revenue-neutral gas tax should not create a short-term negative impact on the economy. It wouldn't raise taxes overall, but just redistribute where taxes are paid—on carbon consumption.

But an interesting question arises: why would voters support CAFE standards or enhanced fuel-efficiency mandates for vehicles (which I discuss in the next section) but oppose gas taxes, even though studies underscore their value?[37] If short-term thinking prevailed, wouldn't we expect the public to oppose both of them equally? Not exactly, and the explanation touches on more nuanced findings. Numerous studies have shown that people behave more impulsively—spending more, saving less, and often preferring items they *want* over items they cognitively believe they *need*—when outcomes are more immediate.[38] Katherine Milkman, Todd Rogers, and Max Bazerman conducted a series of studies showing that people are more likely to select *should* policies (e.g., increased taxes on fossil fuels, increased charitable spending, etc.) when they will be implemented in the distant future rather than in the near future.[39]

Gas taxes pose an immediate impact, while CAFE standards represent a future challenge because they are slated to take effect over many years. And people are more willing to take pain if it is more abstract and occurs in the future.

## CAFE Standards

The Energy Policy Conservation Act, enacted into law by Congress in 1975, established CAFE standards for passenger cars and light trucks. Not retroactive and applicable only to new vehicles, CAFE standards are the fleet-average fuel economy that motor manufacturers must achieve or pay a fine for every vehicle sold that failed to meet the standard. A key goal was to double the 1974 passenger car fuel economy average by 1985 (to 27.5 mpg), and then aim to increase it thereafter. It never happened.

The fuel economy of the average new passenger vehicle peaked in 1988, and through 2010 averaged around 22 mpg for cars and trucks under 8,501 pounds. The Energy Independence and Security Act of 2007 raised fuel economy standards for passenger cars and light trucks to 35 mpg by 2020, the first statutory increase since they had been established in 1975. Since 2009, the Obama administration has accelerated the introduction of tougher fuel economy standards and sought to extend them to heavier vehicles. The first standards covered model years 2012–16 and ultimately required an average fuel economy standard of 35.5 mpg in 2016, surpassing the CAFE law passed by Congress in 2007, which required an average fuel economy of 35 mpg in 2020.

More notably, President Obama in July 2011 signed an agreement with thirteen major automakers to increase fuel economy to 54.5 mpg for cars and light-duty trucks by model year 2025. The president was joined by BMW, Chrysler, Ford, GM, Honda, Hyundai, Jaguar/Land Rover, Kia, Mazda, Mitsubishi, Nissan, Toyota, and Volvo—which together account for more than ninety percent of all vehicles sold in the United States—as well as by the United Auto Workers and the state of California. According to the White House, by 2025 these standards will reduce oil consumption by 2.2 million barrels a day, or as much as half of the oil we import from OPEC every day.

The history of CAFE standards offers mixed evidence of short-term thinking. On the one hand, initial targets were not reached, and for decades little had been done to raise these standards. Congress and the president, partly because they faced a short election cycle and other pressures, were reluctant to move on it, and voters were lukewarm at best. Things changed under Bush and especially under Obama, however, partly due to a unique set of circumstances where automakers had been bailed out by the government during the great recession of 2008 and felt pressure to reciprocate, and perhaps also because they learned Americans will buy efficient vehicles when gas prices climb as they did in 2007–8. Another possible reason for the success of CAFE standards is that, as suggested above, the public now supports them. A poll from the Pew Clean Energy Program found that eighty-two percent of national voters support an increased fuel-efficiency standard of 56 mpg by 2025, with sixty-eight percent strongly favoring the new higher standard.

Yet CAFE standards are only a partial solution for decreasing oil dependence. Why? They affect only new vehicles. They also encourage drivers to drive more due to lower operating costs, which limits the savings of overall consumption and exhaust emissions. CAFE standards also raise the cost of vehicles, meaning buyers are less likely to purchase them, which partly explains why CAFE vehicles have a market share of only three to four percent.[40] While it's difficult to predict how consumers will react to CAFE regulations, the fact is that the public has largely demanded bigger automobiles.

## Buying Fuel-Efficient Vehicles

If decreasing oil use in transportation is critical, one way to do so is to get large numbers of consumers to buy more efficient vehicles. Raising fuel economy standards will push auto companies to make more fuel-efficient vehicles, but consumers still must choose to buy them. To what extent are consumers not buying fuel-efficient vehicles in significant numbers because they are short-term thinkers? That's a challenging question to answer, but consider the following.

Like increased gas taxes, buying a fuel-efficient vehicle represents immediate financial pain. These vehicles tend to cost more, and consumers prefer not to spend more money now even if it means saving money in the long run. According to a Johnson Controls consumer survey, most mainstream consumers will not buy a fuel-efficient vehicle until they become cheaper than traditional cars, and the savings would need to be experienced almost immediately. The data show that seventy-five percent of car owners would consider a more fuel-efficient vehicle when shopping for a new car. But only twenty percent of them are willing to purchase a hybrid, start-stop, or electric vehicle at current gasoline prices hovering between $3.50 and $4.00 per gallon. Consumers will likely take action only when gas prices hit somewhere between $4.00 and $5.00 a gallon.[41] For buyers who focused on economic value, one study based on a review of national survey data found that on average consumers said they expected a return on "investment" in higher fuel economy in 2.9 years, even though they expected to own vehicles, on average, for more than five years.[42] Another study found that the time period during which consumers expected to recoup the added cost of a fuel-efficient vehicle is even shorter, at one and a half to two years.[43]

While some buyers react to higher gas prices by buying more fuel-efficient cars, some studies find that many buyers of these vehicles act for symbolic or ideological reasons, more than for economic value. Interviews reveal that hybrid buyers consider the high price of gasoline, new technologies, national security, the future, the environment, and a new set of values.[44] Matthew Kahn found a correlation between the adoption of hybrid vehicles and the percentage of registered Green Party voters in California.[45] These buyers tended to be longer-term thinkers. One in-depth case study found that these individuals are driven by symbolic meanings, and these symbols tend to deal with longer-range goals. Some buyers see themselves as protecting their families' futures through reduced pollution and oil use; others see a chance to strike out against oil producers and other symbols of the oil era.[46]

Short-term thinking is also related to larger problems. The hard-core hybrid buyers are motivated by longer-run ideological concerns at least as much as by gas money savings. But what about other buyers? For them, a gas tax could spur purchases of more efficient vehicles. It could keep prices at a predictably high level, making producers and consumers more likely to embrace efficient vehicles, while spurring competition in electric motorization and biofuels. But, as discussed above, American politicians reject raising taxes, as do most citizens. Short-term thinking, in other words, impedes the ability to incentivize such purchases.

Getting America into electric vehicles runs into other challenges related to short-term thinking. We would have to develop an infrastructure for the use of such vehicles, and at present it's not clear who and which institutions would support such a longer-term venture. Recharging stations would be needed around the country so that drivers could use their vehicles to reach distant destinations. There is no point in building electric cars if consumers are afraid to buy them for fear of getting stranded. We must also have appropriate power sources to run these vehicles. Otherwise, electricity demand may eventually outstrip supply—a problem that already exists in America. The key options for producing electricity are natural gas, nuclear, solar, wind, and coal. Finally, we also need a more efficient and connected national electrical grid to efficiently run electric cars. In part, this will make it easier to transport and share electricity nationally. So, for instance, if solar power is not producing enough electricity in Ohio, nuclear or wind power from elsewhere can make up for it.

But who will build this infrastructure? Without longer-run incentives, the private sector has understandably acted in its own interests. And government support is hobbled by a variety of pressures, in both the short and long term, including budget problems. If increasing the numbers of electric cars is in the long-term interest for the country—a rational choice for America—we currently lack the mechanisms to reach that goal.

Who will build large numbers of electric vehicles for consumers to buy en masse? It might be that automobile companies are reluctant, fearing a drop in stock price that could break what some traders see as key technical levels, causing an even steeper price drop. Some might say that focusing on the short-term bottom line is rational, but even assuming that building a fleet of electric cars could mean increased risks, short-term thinking can produce negative results in the long run. The bankruptcies of GM and Chrysler, for example, resulted from many factors, but among them was the possibility that they were slow to adjust to future realities, where efficient vehicles would gain in importance as oil prices soared and as environmental concerns became more prominent. Significant change requires significant long-term planning. Still, quarterly financial statements often drive decisions in the auto industry, even though a similar strategy almost bankrupted the industry and delayed the introduction of hybrid and electric models that could gain market share.

## High-Speed Rail

High-speed rail is an important part of the solution to the problem of oil dependence, but it has not been embraced significantly in the United States, partly because of budgetary constraints, doubts about its investment potential compared to other forms of transportation, and possibly short-term thinking.

Building high-speed rail requires long-term planning. It needs significant up-front capital investment for projects that could take years to pay off or that might not produce an economic payoff but decreases oil dependence. The same is true of every new infrastructure project. When Central Pacific built the western part of the transcontinental railroad, the U.S. government provided financing in the form of land grants and the ability to issue bonds. The federal government paid for the interstate highway system that supported the rise of the American automobile culture.

As part of his first term agenda, President Barack Obama jump-started investment in high-speed rail. On February 17, 2009, the American Recovery and Reinvestment Act was signed into law, and it included $8 billion for intercity and high-speed rail projects. Congress supplemented the initial $8 billion with additional appropriations, and the administration aimed for greater authorization of $53 billion for high-speed rail over the six years from fiscal year 2012 through 2017. But opposition to high-speed rail emerged from budgetary questions. Given the fiscal plight of states and the growing federal deficit, governments alone probably cannot finance ten high-speed corridors that could ultimately cost a total of $200 billion or more. The creative use of private capital will be needed to proceed.

The fundamental choice facing the United States is about the longer-term future. Decisions made today about transportation will shape the American landscape and economy for decades. Even the most farsighted planners of the interstate highway system did not anticipate the extent to which the new roads they built would help spawn a burgeoning suburbia. High-speed rail could produce positive results, but only if built in the right places with high population densities, among other things. Imagine traveling from New York to Philadelphia in a fraction of the time it takes to drive and without the security checks, the clogged terminals, and flight cancellations that plague air travel these days. What if, over the longer run, you could also save money, substantially decrease pollution and the need to build expensive highways, and create American jobs while you were at it? The technology is already here, but it's underrated, underutilized, and often overlooked. The United States is far behind other developed nations in developing its high-speed rail infrastructure, ranking eighth in miles of rail in operation, eighth in miles under construction, sixth in miles planned, and ninth in total miles, according to data reported by the International Union of Railways in 2011.[47]

Around the world, high-speed trains have roundly beaten planes on price, overall travel time, and convenience at ranges of up to six hundred miles. Consider what happened in Europe: commercial flights all but disappeared after high-speed trains were established between Paris and Lyon. And in the first year of operation, a high-speed link between Madrid and Barcelona cut the air travel market by about fifty percent.

In Asia, China has seen the light. It plans to build forty-two high-speed rail lines across thirteen thousand kilometers (some eight thousand miles) in the next three years. America spent $13 billion in stimulus funds for high-speed rail, while China is spending $556 billion on a rail construction plan that will link nearly all its provincial cities *in the next five years*. The Shanghai–Beijing link alone is expected to create half a million jobs. The Chinese Railway Ministry says that rail can transport 160 million people per year, compared with eighty million for a four-lane highway. In addition to the central goal of decreasing oil use and pollution, China seeks to bolster its economy with investment in rail and also to satisfy the demands for mobility by its growing middle class.

For America, as fewer people opt for gas-guzzling air or car travel, a high-speed rail system would hit U.S. oil dependence right where it counts: in the gas tank. High-speed rail is most economical in areas of high population and, more importantly, high population densities. In August 2009, Nobel Prize–winning economist Paul Krugman argued that America has a "bigger potential market for fast rail than any European country."[48]

A few states, such as Florida, are actively considering the viability of high-speed rail. Yet only California has made noticeable strides, with notable cost overruns possibly due to ineffective implementation. In November 2008, California voters supported $10 billion in funding for a rail system linking Los Angeles and

San Francisco with trains capable of traveling 220 miles per hour, cutting travel time via Interstate 5 from about six hours to just two and a half hours. Much study is needed to understand why California faced significant cost overruns. Additional studies could also help determine the best places to build high-speed rail versus other forms of efficient transportation. But it appears that rail works well in other parts of the world, and there is no reason to believe that it cannot be an important part of America's comprehensive energy policy, too.

## Speed Limits

Some analysts argue that reducing speed limits may be the easiest and simplest way to improve fuel efficiency. Fuel economy decreases two percent for each one-mile increase above sixty miles per hour.[49] The Paris-based International Energy Agency (IEA) has found that eco-driving, which includes maintaining speed limits, can reduce fuel use by up to twenty percent for some drivers and possibly as much as ten percent on average across all drivers on a lasting basis. Consider that the United States imports around fifteen percent of its oil per year from the Middle East. In theory, eco-driving could eliminate the need for a good portion of these imports. The IEA is encouraging all countries to develop eco-driving programs that are appropriate for their national circumstances, including speed limits below seventy-five miles per hour—a point where fuel efficiency drops significantly in most vehicles.

The United States took measures to decrease oil dependence in response to the oil crisis of 1973–74, but the actions were short lived. In March 1974, Congress established a national speed limit of fifty-five miles per hour. Congress strictly enforced the law by withholding federal highway money to states that did not comply. Noncompliance was eventually defined as having more than fifty percent of interstate highway traffic traveling at speeds greater than fifty-five miles per hour for two successive years. In the mid-1980s, Arizona, Maryland, New Hampshire, Vermont, and Wyoming were all found in noncompliance and either received warnings from the Department of Transportation or were penalized with a loss of federal highway funds.

The national speed limit did not last long. As part of the 1987 highway funding bill, Congress permitted states to raise their speed limits on certain interstates from fifty-five to sixty-five miles per hour. This action was taken in part because of falling gasoline prices—and thus the reduced need to save energy—and in part as a result of widespread noncompliance with the mandatory federal speed limit. But it was not until December 1995 that the 1974 speed limit law was repealed entirely by the new Republican majority in Congress. Despite loud opposition from safety, medical, and insurance groups, the Senate repealed the federal speed limit law by a vote of eighty to sixteen, and the House bill was passed by unanimous consent. It is worth emphasizing that by repealing the federal speed limit, Congress did not raise speed limits in the states. It allowed states to raise the speed limits as they saw fit.

## Short-Term Thinking and Rationality

Cognitive biases like the short-term bias can impede the ability to consider options carefully, producing aspects of irrational decision making. Judging rationality depends on whose rationality is in question and on what time horizon, which leaves us with different outcomes. At times, short-term thinking can be clearly irrational, such as when the decision maker does not consider the longer-run costs. Drug addictions come to mind. Taking illegal drugs may be fun for a quick high, but it is disastrous as a long-term habit.

Sometimes, however, short-term thinking can be quite rational in the near term for individuals or organizations. Polluting and wasting energy is cheaper and easier for individuals than not polluting or conserving energy. Yet what is rational for the individual or organization in the short term may well be irrational for society in the longer term. As Steven Yaffe stresses, environmental problems emerge from a number of dynamics, including the tendency to privilege short-term rationality over long-term rationality.[50] In some areas of energy, the best strategy for the individual produces the worst outcome for the collective. This dynamic has the trappings of what Garret Hardin originally referred to as the "tragedy of the commons"—an idea that has gone through multiple incarnations since Hardin's formulation.[51]

The theoretical notion of the tragedy of the commons is simple but salient, lending it some fidelity and explanatory power. It assumes that there is a resource open to all—the commons—over which no actor has control or property rights. Rational actors seek to exploit this resource because the benefits of exploitation exceed the costs, and the actor can gain without having to share any or much of the benefits.[52] Even if the actor acts as a responsible citizen and decides not to exploit the resource, she will still have to pay a similar amount to deal with the problems generated by the exploitation of the resource by others. Good behavior is not rewarded with fewer costs. If we multiply such calculations among all of the salient actors, the end result becomes the "tragedy of the commons."[53]

Since Hardin published his piece, a literature has arisen that challenges his bleak outlook about self-interested actors caught in a tragic trap of their own shortsightedness. This literature has shown that groups can create norms and arrangements that limit exploitation and conserve shared resources.[54]

Nonetheless, Hardin's theory still offers important insights, especially into the critical area of global oil dependence. Oil is a resource that carries with it the potential of the "tragedy of the commons," unless greater coordinated actions are taken to preempt this outcome. Most rational egoists tend to use oil in a manner that satisfies their economic and political interests, even if their behavior contributes to a growing problem for the commons. They do so because, at least in the short term, it is far less costly than taking measures to decrease oil dependence. And even if they spent significant time, energy, and political capital to take serious measures to decrease oil consumption, they would still have to pay a similar cost to deal with the effects of exploiting oil, provided that others continued to behave as they always have. These dynamics may not be rational for the state insofar as they impeded careful consideration of options to maximize national interest.

## The Status Quo Bias

While this chapter focuses on the short-term bias, it also applies two more biases to illuminate challenges to decreasing oil dependence. Many studies reveal a status quo bias,[55] in fields ranging from economics, where it has been used to explain opposition to trade reform,[56] to political science and impeding human enhancement writ large.[57] This bias refers to the idea that established behaviors, such as those related to energy, do not change without significant incentive.[58] The status quo bias can be characterized as a cognitive error, where one option is incorrectly judged to be better than another because it represents the status quo. Psychologists call this a "comfort zone" bias on the basis of research suggesting that breaking from the status quo is, for most people, emotionally uncomfortable. While different explanations exist for this bias, some argue that it increases (in relative terms) with the number of choice alternatives, and may be best explained as a psychological anchor: the stronger the individual's previous commitment to the status quo, the stronger the anchoring effect.[59]

The status quo bias is different from the short-term bias. Short-term bias doesn't prevent change from happening; it just produces change based on short-term thinking and behavior. Meanwhile, the status quo bias forestalls change. It reflects how people tend not to change behavior unless the incentive to change is strong, and how they are often more concerned about the risk of change than about the risk of not changing. Daniel Kahneman, Jack Knetsch, and Richard Thaler created experiments that could produce this effect reliably.[60] When combined, the short-term and the status quo biases challenge longer-term thinking and behavior, which require change in action. It can be hard to establish that a status quo bias exists in energy policy and behavior, but some studies show that people overvalue the status quo. For example, California electric power consumers were asked about their preferences regarding trade-offs between service reliability and rates. The respondents fell into two groups, one receiving much more reliable service than the other. Each group was asked to state a preference among six combinations of reliability and rates, with one of the combinations designated as the status quo. "The results demonstrated a pronounced status quo bias. In the high reliability group, 60.2 percent selected their status quo as their first choice, while only 5.7 percent expressed a preference for the low reliability option currently being experienced by the other group, though it came with a 30 percent reduction in rates. The low reliability group, however, quite liked their status quo, 58.3 percent ranking it first. Only 5.8 percent of this group selected the high reliability option at a proposed 30 percent rate increase in rates."[61]

There are often good reasons for leaving things unchanged. The grass, as they say, is not always greener on the other side. What's important is to judge when a status quo bias is impeding clear reflection on the value of different options.

## Prospect Theory and Crises

The status quo bias is related to prospect theory, a theory for which there is much experimental evidence. Prospect theory can help explain why U.S. energy policy changed during crises, but then tended to return to the status quo once those crises were over. It assumes that people value gains and losses differently, even if they have the same value. If asked to make a decision about an issue—but in one instance the outcome was expressed in terms of possible gains and the other was expressed in term of possible losses—a person will choose the outcome with possible gains, even if the gains and losses are exactly the same. Rational approaches would assume no difference in choice.

The loss-aversion part of prospect theory in particular is one of the most robust experimental biases ever discovered.[62] In the study of foreign policy, prospect theory suggests that decision makers will take greater risks when things are going poorly and will be risk averse when things are going well. But such actions don't conform with rational behavior. Scholars have sought to apply prospect theory to international relations at a general or theoretical level.[63] Jeffrey Taliaferro argues that when leaders perceive losses, they tend to initiate risky diplomatic or military intervention, continuing to take such risks even if failure looms because they want to recoup losses.[64] Other scholars have illuminated prospect theory in more specific events such as President Roosevelt and the Munich crisis,[65] as well as the Cuban missile crisis.[66]

Prospect theory may offer insight into U.S. energy policy. It may help explain why policy evolved during crises and why subsequent risks were taken. As examples, the 1973 Arab oil embargo launched the numerous actions discussed earlier in this chapter. The 9/11 attack and the wars it motivated increased concern about oil dependency and contributed to the 2005 and 2007 energy acts. And changes in policy even occurred beyond the executive branch. The U.S. military has sought to cut its dependence on foreign oil for decades, but 9/11, two wars in the Middle East, and the oil price spike of 2008 (when oil reached around $147 per barrel) spurred it to take additional action. Secretary of the Navy Ray Mabus accelerated the service's shift to alternative energy with a very ambitious program that included developing a "green" strike group made up of nuclear-powered carriers, hybrid-electric-driven surface ships (their oil supplemented by biofuel), and biofuel aircraft. The Navy now aims by 2015 to cut the use of petroleum by half in its fifty-thousand-vehicle fleet by incorporating hybrid and electric vehicles. Military leaders do not have the same constraints as elected officials, business owners, or civilian car owners, so they are not as vulnerable to the short-term thinking bias (although they sometimes exhibit status quo thinking).

Crises may help eclipse short-term thinking in another way. Crises can change the dynamic of the tragedy of the commons insofar as they make us believe more in a common problem that requires collective action. With the stakes high, egoistic behavior may yield in some measure to thinking about the whole, the greater good, and the steps needed to protect that good.

Prospect theory is useful, but future work on its relation to U.S. energy policy is needed to see how energy actors perceive to what extent things are not going well against a baseline of what "well" really is for them. That can help us judge levels of risk taking that the theory predicts, but it is not easy to do. As Jack Levy has put it, prospect theory offers some novel and theoretically interesting hypotheses about foreign policy and international relations, but actually testing it poses various conceptual and methodological problems.[67]

## America versus Other Countries

If cognitive biases play a role, shouldn't we expect these biases to apply across the board? Why does America lag other countries in dealing with oil dependence? First, we can debate how advanced other countries are in decreasing oil dependence, as certainly some countries are more dependent on oil than others. But even if it's not just an American problem, it seems that the United States suffers more from short-term thinking about energy issues than some other countries, such as the Netherlands, which has achieved much higher fuel economy. Why?

The countries with the lowest oil dependence appear to be socialistic. Their citizens may have short-term biases, but these can be overcome by an emphasis on the collective or socialism or high taxes for government services. The culture of individualism in America promotes consumer behavior and unregulated markets compared to China or even Europe. Americans privilege freedom and have a greater antigovernment sentiment than people in other countries. The American consumer is stronger relative to the government than citizens of China, Japan, or Europe. And consumers are often focused more on the short term than governments. China has five- and ten-year plans. It sets the energy policy looking deep into the future. Socialist economies are more willing to use public funds for government projects, including high-speed rail and solar works. They can raise taxes or draw on them for such projects more easily than in the tax-averse United States. And they tend to accept short-term losses for longer-run gains as part of the societal welfare net.

Of course, socialism has a strong downside, as the recent European debt crisis and recession have demonstrated, but something can be learned about European approaches to decreasing oil dependence. At the same time, such energy strategies need to be consistent with capitalist practices that unleash American innovation and boost economic growth.

## Conclusion

America is not just addicted to oil. It is addicted to cheap oil, and it could more easily decrease its dependence if its leaders and citizens conceptualized the problem at least in part as a short-term bias. As Jay Hakes has noted, America won the war with oil dependence in the 1970s after the Arab oil embargo, but there is "one problem with winning a war. People soon want to settle back to life as usual, and complacency sets in."[68]

While global oil dependence may smack of a tragedy of the commons, it need not be so.[69] Nobel Prize winner Elinor Ostrom has intelligently argued and elaborated upon this notion.[70] In her view, it is a mistake to believe (and some evidence questions the raw notion) that actors dealing with dilemmas of the commons are trapped in an inextricable problem driven by unrelenting and unavoidable egoism.[71] But what can be done to deal with this short-term bias? It is beyond the present scope to sketch such a policy and conceptualization. In basic terms, however, people often vary substantially in the degree to which they exhibit short-term thinking. It depends on context, the type of decision, and issue area. It seems fair to say that short-term thinking is especially dangerous, with problems that build over the longer run and don't go away easily. They require baby steps to solve, each offering little instant gratification but building toward a longer-run solution. The goal, then, appears to be to identify what types of small steps will eventually accumulate to reduce our heavy consumption of oil, and then put in motion policies to incentivize that those steps be taken en masse. By doing so, policy makers and political leaders can eventually turn around the limitations of short-term bias, instituting change for longer-term solutions.

# Conclusion

## Making Better Decisions

---

Leaders, professors, doctors, plumbers—all people—have something in common. They want to make good decisions, but in doing so they sometimes face obstacles that originate in how their minds work. These mental errors or cognitive biases, which often work at the subconscious level, sometimes derail decisions and produce bad results. Overconfidence, for instance, is not something about which we are often aware. People don't say, "Hey, I'm going to take this action even though I'm overconfident about my prospects for success." They don't walk down the aisle saying, "I'm overconfident about the success of this marriage, but what the heck." People usually think that they will succeed and maybe even live happily ever after.

All of us can benefit from exploring how to make better decisions. Even the smartest among us sometimes engage in poor decision making, and according to one prominent study even more so under certain conditions,[1] and we have seen our leaders make poor decisions time and again, sometimes costing lives and billions of dollars. This book has underscored how cognitive biases can cloud the way people perceive themselves, others, and the world around them. In over fifty years of research, dozens of different biases have been identified and categorized, including biases that distort our judgments, introduce errors into our estimates, and contribute to wrong choices.

Remarkably, while much work has been done on identifying cognitive biases, much less exists on how to deal with them. This concluding chapter draws primarily on the psychology and foreign policy literature, the analysis of this book, and on my own work on decision making.

The literature suggests that cognitive biases have a negative impact on decision making,[2] a finding that many political scientists would support. Better decision making is especially important for policy makers. As political scientists

Mark Schafer and Scott Crichlow show, certain decision-making techniques and practices limit the ability of policy makers to meet their goals and advance the national interest, indicating that successful policy often depends on the quality of the decision-making process itself.[3] And cognitive biases can produce not just poor outcomes but dramatic consequences. Daniel Kahneman and Jonathan Renshon argue, partly on the basis of past psychological research, that when it comes to the question of war, cognitive biases of how people process information and evaluate risk predispose political leaders to take military action over diplomatic solutions. Such impulses "incline national leaders to exaggerate the evil intentions of adversaries, to misjudge how adversaries perceive them, to be overly sanguine when hostilities start, and overly reluctant to make necessary concessions in negotiations. In short, these biases have the effect of making wars more likely to begin and more difficult to end."[4]

It is important to understand not just that cognitive biases are at work, but also *how* they work. Academics sometimes assume that people are rational in making decisions. It may be a useful assumption in building models of human and state behavior, and may explain important dimensions of any case, but it can also carry costs. Failing to account for cognitive biases can leave us with blind spots about how individuals and states make decisions and—with regard to the issues discussed in this book—about the decisions that shaped U.S. energy and foreign policy. So how can individuals, be they foreign policy leaders or laypeople, diminish the role of cognitive biases so as to enhance their chances of success? This chapter offers steps to address the cognitive biases examined in this book as well as some other related biases.

Debiasing techniques are sometimes recommended to deal with cognitive biases and are usually specific to the bias in consideration and even to the individual (academic experts, students, foreign leaders, etc.). For this reason, techniques to deal with overconfidence differ from those aimed at decreasing confirmation bias.

I cover the complex literature on debiasing in a readable manner, drawing on advice that is sensitive to real-life conditions. We must consider that decision makers of all stripes (but especially those in government) are sometimes under time constraints and cannot take forever to collect and weigh all the evidence. Nor can they be entirely free of constraints imposed by bureaucracy, the chain of command, dependence on other thinkers, and protocol. It would be great if we could turn decision makers into error-free robots, but alas life has different ideas for us all. Even with all their challenges, not all cognitive biases are created equal. Some may actually enable faster decisions, while others decrease rationality. In addition, no broad theory exists for why cognitive biases occur, which could allow us to identify some broad solutions. A 2012 article suggested that at least eight seemingly unrelated biases can result from noisy information processing during storage and retrieval of information in human memory.[5]

What follows are suggestions for dealing with some central cognitive biases. We start with formalized procedures for decision making after first discussing what debiasing can reasonably achieve.

## What Can Debiasing Achieve?

It may appear to the layperson or even to decision makers unfamiliar with work on cognitive biases that avoiding biases just requires being aware of them. It's reasonable to assume that if we know a tendency toward overconfidence exists, we can avoid it by displaying greater humility in our assessments and predictions. There is some truth in this idea. Self-awareness can be important to debiasing, but it is not enough, partly because some cognitive biases emerge from subconscious impulses, or because bias may be hardwired or socialized into our mental frameworks. Even if others point out our overconfidence, we are likely to reject their warnings, assuming that there is something wrong with them or their perception. We all know someone whose subconscious impulses both lead him astray and make it hard for him to see the errors of his ways, no matter what we say.

But researchers debate the extent to which purely cognitive strategies can improve reasoning. The optimists are sometimes referred to as meliorists; they believe that reasoning can be improved through experience and education, whereas apologists are more pessimistic about the computational constraints and unconscious impulses that are hard to rectify.[6] Wherever one stands, most debiasing techniques are designed largely to shift cognitive processing from what is referred to as a System 1 mode of thinking (automatic, heuristic) to a System 2 mode of thinking (controlled, governed by rules). The first system is preconscious, automatic, fast, unreflective, and slow to change, while the second is conscious, slow, reflective, and flexible. The vast majority of decisions are made through System 1, which draws heavily on emotions and often trumps the rule-governed, reasoned System 2, making it difficult for the second system to educate the first.[7]

In addition to implementing cognitive strategies to achieve debiasing, another approach is to use strategies that are external to the decision maker. External decision-making strategies include developing formal procedures for rational decision making, improving information processing, making group decisions, and employing computers, graphics, logic, and statistical models. Some thinkers put greater stock in external decision-making strategies because to some extent they bypass the challenges of trying to change how people think, instead changing the conditions that affect their thinking.

Before forging ahead, I should point out that while some of my recommendations for improving decision making are drawn from the foreign policy literature and from my own work, the debiasing approaches I discuss in this chapter are drawn from the psychology literature. Psychologists usually obtain their results from individual-level study under experimental conditions, which may raise some questions about their applicability to foreign policy. Foreign policy is a complex process that involves individuals, groups, bureaucracies, and other countries, and it is conducted under real-life conditions. Nonetheless, I believe that suggestions from the psychology literature can be useful for the layperson as well as for individuals in government.

Even so, we must not be overconfident with regard to what debiasing can achieve. There are no magic bullets for avoiding mental errors, but there are a variety of approaches that can reduce their impact.

## Institute Formal Procedures for Rational Decision Making

As suggested above, one approach is not to debias individuals directly but rather to create external conditions that make biases less prominent. Some might argue that cognitive biases are hard to eliminate, but formal procedures that encourage rational decision making can help as an external approach.

We consider actors, whether individuals or countries, to be rational if they identify options, carefully weigh the costs and benefits of various options, and then choose (or try to choose) the option that best advances national interests.[8] These procedures can serve as a partial antidote to some of the mental errors that individuals sometimes make. For instance, studies show that people who are more open to contradictory evidence tend to make more accurate predictions.[9] Instituting rationality procedures is especially important for decision makers in government, whose actions potentially carry great weight. Leaders don't have the time to get stuck in overthinking; the real trick may be to consider the options well enough to understand them, and then to decide.

Leaders and even laypeople would be well advised to use such procedures for purposes of generating and evaluating alternative options for problem solving, and for engaging in all the tasks that are necessary for doing so.[10] Unfortunately, alternative options are often neglected. As a notable exception, President John F. Kennedy's decision-making group during the 1962 Cuban missile crisis followed a careful process at the president's urging, laying out at least ten alternatives and analyzing them methodically.[11]

The following formalized procedures for encouraging a rational process of decision making can help. First, at a basic level, it is vital to identify sensible options. Jonathan Baron argues that better thinking results if we expand the search phase before making decisions. Doing so generates more alternatives and helps collect better information for judging between these alternatives. It isn't specifically about debiasing, but expanding one's search may have a significant debiasing effect.[12] Formal procedures can prevent certain alternatives from being rejected before being considered, and prevent other options from being adopted more quickly than is optimal.

Second, maintaining an open, free-flowing context for ideas and views is critical. It is also challenging. The culture of an organization can cause people to favor or resist the automatic use of unexamined biases. Take the case of the safety culture at the National Aeronautic and Space Administration (NASA) in the first decade of the twenty-first century. In contrast to NASA's previous approaches, disagreements were increasingly encouraged, pushing NASA to create a far more open environment that helped produce safer space missions.[13] Studies show how important it is to remain open to alternative views, but the question arises as to how this can be accomplished.

All individuals need to be aware of pressures toward conformity and like-minded thinking. Leaders in particular need to confront such inclinations, creating an environment that rewards new ideas. They should encourage others to develop arguments and counterarguments for each option, rather than simply promoting one option or version of it, and should ensure as complete an airing of views on the options as is possible. Sometimes, even subtle comments can indicate to group members that they must agree with their leaders. A high-ranking member of the group might jokingly call an innovative thinker a trouble-maker, leading others to believe that novel thinking will be quietly penalized. Or she might respond to a counter idea or argument by saying that the group needs to stay on focus and not deviate from the topic at hand. Leaders need to allow dissent to surface, so that creative ideas can be expressed without fear of criticism or even tacit or explicit retribution. Various approaches can help accomplish these goals, including using formal rational procedures, tapping outside experts, encouraging debate, playing "devil's advocate," and brainstorming or generating ideas without restriction.

Following the Bay of Pigs disaster in Cuba, which was driven by a seemingly unanimous confidence among John Kennedy's advisers, Robert Kennedy suggested to his brother that a devil's advocate should thereafter always be present to give an opposing opinion.[14] The intuitive logic behind introducing a devil's advocate is evident, but its implementation is complex, partly because the role of devil's advocate must be empowered by a leader who may marginalize a true dissenter (such as President Johnson reportedly did to Undersecretary of State George Ball).[15] Leaders should try to avoid such tendencies, as difficult as that may be.

Third, one must list the costs and benefits for each option by consulting others, including colleagues and outside experts. Inclusive decision making allows for greater consideration of information and options, and should take into consideration the views of analysts who are not specialists in the subject matter and who may ask unique questions, as well as assess the argumentation, internal consistency, logic, and relationship of the evidence to the conclusion. Some scholars advocate a "multiple advocacy" structure to ensure that multiple actors and views are formally integrated into the process, and argue that the conditions necessary for a multiple advocacy system to work are difficult to achieve but worth considering.

Unlike the multiple advocacy approach, the devil's advocate approach describes a role, not a complete structure of decision making. In multiple advocacy, (1) advocates should exhibit an "adequate degree of diversity of views"—there are no major discrepancies in the distribution of power (influence), competence and information (relevant to a given policy issue), analytical resources, and bargaining/persuasion skills; (2) there should be presidential-level participation to monitor and regulate the advocacy process; and (3) there should be sufficient time for adequate debate and "give and take."[16] Whatever the exact approach, gaining multiple inputs into decision making is important. The 2003 decision to go to war in Iraq, for example, did not consider multiple advocacy. As this book has shown, there appears to have been no meeting at which the options were identified and weighed. Quite the contrary: the evidence and the descriptions of those involved suggest that President Bush made his final decision either on his own or with just one or two other advisers, even though his decision was probably based on significant prior discussions and briefings.

Fourth, a wide information search is important. Policy makers perceive and access information in a number of ways. These perceptions can in turn determine how information is gathered, processed, and framed, which in turn affects foreign policy. Missing data are normal in decision-making arenas such as in the intelligence community, but it is probably more difficult to recognize that critical information is absent. As an antidote, analysts should identify explicitly those variables on which information is lacking and their relative importance, consider competing hypotheses on why information is missing or unclear, and then modify their judgment—and especially confidence in their judgment—accordingly.

Fifth, work on joint versus separate decision making suggests that people can move from suboptimal System 1 thinking toward improved System 2 thinking when they consider and choose simultaneously between multiple options rather than by separately accepting or rejecting options.[17] People seem to exhibit less willpower when they weigh choices separately rather than jointly,[18] suggesting that considering multiple options together may allow people to see the bigger picture as opposed to their own particular interests.

Sixth, delaying decisions can prove useful, if time allows. Research indicates that our first impulses tend to be more emotional than logical.[19] Any change in a decision's context that promotes System 2 thinking has the potential to reduce common biases resulting from impulsiveness. As political scientist Janice Gross Stein argues, leaders who are aware of cognitive dynamics can call for compulsory delays that leave time for reflection and analysis and expose themselves to counterarguments. They can demand worst-case scenarios and anticipate how they would respond. Such actions can help avoid impulsive, emotion-driven choices.[20] Decision makers can be pushed to ask themselves, "What are some reasons my initial judgment might be wrong?"[21]

Seventh, Renshon has suggested using "guided self-reflection" aimed at uncovering and tracing as many connections within the decision makers' policy thinking as possible and at making decision makers aware of them. Guided self-reflection requires attention to at least two levels. The first would include how leaders gather and organize information relevant to solving particular problems, including identifying the problem, how it can be conceived, the appropriate frame of analysis, and the implications of different options. The second would look more closely at leaders' beliefs, assumptions, and inferences as they proceed through the process of reaching a decision about the policy.[22]

The approaches discussed above can help deal with most of the cognitive biases discussed in this book and examined below. But some special approaches are useful for each particular bias.

## Diminishing Overconfidence

Evidence suggests that the 2003 Iraq War decision was marked by overconfidence, which can arise from numerous factors. These factors may be difficult to identify and address, particularly ideology, religion, and even high testosterone levels, which are rooted in neurology.[23] But such handicaps notwithstanding, several approaches can help diminish overconfidence.

One System 2 strategy is to take an outsider's perspective, which involves removing oneself mentally from a specific situation or considering the class of decisions to which the current problem belongs. Doing so has been shown to reduce decision makers' overconfidence about the depth of their knowledge and the time required to complete a task.[24]

Research has also shown that simply encouraging people to "consider the opposite" of whatever decision they are about to make can reduce errors in judgment by lessening decision biases such as overconfidence.[25] Analysts can use counterfactual reasoning to push experts to consider worst-case scenarios.[26] The strategy of considering opposing viewpoints consists of nothing more than asking what might be wrong with one's view. Similarly, studies show that prompting decision makers to consider alternative hypotheses can reduce confirmation biases when seeking and assessing new information, because it directs attention to contrary evidence that would not otherwise be considered.[27]

Worst-case scenario planning and a full vetting of opposing views can be achieved in foreign policy decision making or in any enterprise by appreciating the contributions of underlings. In the Iraq War case, the views of lower-ranking group members were not carefully considered, certainly not when it came to the final war decision, which the president appeared to make with limited input. Of course, presidents must sometimes make decisions quickly, and they cannot always elicit advice from all quarters, but there's a good mean between temporizing and not drawing on sensible input. Jonathan Renshon and Stanley Renshon discuss work on another method called the "murder board." Murder boards are a tradition in the U.S. Pentagon, where an experienced committee attempts to find flaws in a plan—something that was absent, for instance, in making decisions about the disastrous Iranian hostage rescue mission in 1980, when the planners reviewed their own product, allowing for positive illusions to cloud judgment.[28] Committees aimed at finding flaws may well temper overconfidence.

Another approach is to deal with a related cognitive bias—the illusion where decision makers believe they can control outcomes that are actually random or determined by chance factors. To address this problem, research suggests that instead of asking people about the probabilities of an event occurring, where the illusion of control can affect their answer, it is better to ask them about frequencies. For example, if an event were to occur one hundred times, on how many occasions would you expect outcome X to occur? Asking such questions can help shatter the illusion of control by underscoring the difficulty of knowing outcomes and by highlighting chance factors.[29] The idea is to change how we think about events; to consider many events rather than one event that we believe we can control.

Since some evidence suggests that people reason more accurately when thinking about frequencies rather than probabilities,[30] we can present information to decision makers as frequencies, thereby debiasing the environment or directly training them to translate probabilistic reasoning tasks into frequency formats.[31]

One study showed that individuals trained in logic and statistics, such as economics professors, were less likely to be influenced by some cognitive biases. They were more likely than biology or humanities professors to report abandoning a consumer activity in which they had "sunk" money, such as going to the movies or eating at restaurants, despite having the same consumption opportunities.[32] As Philip Tetlock shows, people (including foreign policy experts) who make poor calculations of probability are loath to envision the inevitability of error.[33] Experts tend to overestimate the likelihood of war, for example, because they can envision causal pathways to armed conflict, a highly salient occurrence that they have likely studied. They pay less attention to the frequency of wars over an extended period of time.[34]

While ex ante debiasing addresses biases prior to making decisions, another approach is ex post calibration, as used in risk assessment. Some scholars argue the feasibility of a Bayesian calibration process in which actors learn from past errors. For example, if experts mispredict the chances of cooperation, they can learn what caused the error and use those data for calibrating the expert.[35] One promising debiasing technique is to give decision makers cognitive feedback informing them of the discrepancy between their accuracy and their confidence estimate for a particular decision; such repeated feedback can encourage them to reassess their confidence in the situation and can possibly decrease the overconfidence bias.[36] This approach has been used in a wide variety of applications ranging from foreign policy to criminal justice.

## The Planning Fallacy

In the Iraq case, decision makers appeared to be overconfident—a bias that contributed to another bias referred to as the "planning fallacy." Antidotes to overconfidence are described above, but there is one additional approach that could help with overconfidence and especially the planning fallacy. Daniel Kahneman and Amos Tversky discovered a systematic fallacy in planning in which people underestimate the costs, completion times, and risks of planned actions, but they overestimate the benefits of the same actions.[37] Kahneman and Tversky believed that this planning fallacy stemmed from actors taking an "inside view," or focusing on aspects of the specific planned action rather than on the outcomes of similar cases that were already completed, which might have given them more depth in understanding the difficulty of planning in general. On that basis, Kahneman and Tversky recommended that forecasters should "make every effort to frame the forecasting problem so as to facilitate" the use of all information;[38] in other words, they should gather information from many similar cases which will provide a "base rate" or general base of information from which to work.

Such an approach is now called "reference class forecasting," which predicts the future not by projecting from one case, but by looking at similar past situations and their outcomes.[39] Bent Flyvbjerg and the COWI consulting group developed a methodology for reference class forecasting in the areas of policy, planning, and management. At the core, it involves identifying a reference class of past, similar projects, and then comparing that general stock of cases to the specific project in order to assess its prospects.[40] In 2005, the American Planning Association endorsed reference class forecasting and asserted that planners should use it in addition to traditional methods as a way to improve accuracy. Flyvbjerg found that inaccurate projections of costs, demands, and other impacts of plans are a major problem and stem from optimism bias and strategic misrepresentation. He discovered that reference class forecasting helps achieve accuracy in projections by basing them on actual performance in a reference class of comparable actions, thereby bypassing both optimism bias and strategic misrepresentation.[41] In his 2011 book *Thinking, Fast and Slow*, Kahneman called Flyvbjerg's counsel to use reference class forecasting where possible "the single most important piece of advice regarding how to increase accuracy in forecasting."[42]

## Trying Not to Dig a Deeper Hole

Sometimes, instead of learning to adjust our plans, we dig in our heels to defend them, which can be fueled by and contribute to overconfidence. One study revealed that foreign policy experts generally continued to defend their wrong forecasts, and that the more confident they were in their original forecast, the more threatened they were by disconfirming evidence, and the more motivated they were to defend their positions.[43] Such inclinations help us understand what not to do in decision making. In the Iraq case in particular, Bush administration experts argued that the Iraqis failed to seize the opportunity of removing Saddam, rather than considering that their forecast for a democratic Iraq was overconfident. They dug a deeper hole by not carefully assessing their own faults, when doing so might have allowed for quicker correctives to policy errors.

Being aware of this trap of getting sunk in deeper instead of adapting as an event proceeds is important. After all, decision making doesn't end when action is initiated; it often continues to be relevant as events unfold. Sometimes politicians won't admit errors or fail to make adjustments because they believe it will make them look weak, indecisive, and confused. That may be true, but failing to change course can be much worse, and sometimes overconfidence makes decision makers less likely to change.

## Checking Confirmation Bias

Confirmation biases rivet our daily lives, from the personal to the political. The media and politicians themselves have made it easier for extreme partisans to seek confirming information and to screen out disconfirming views.[44] Confirmation biases contribute to overconfidence in personal beliefs and myriad other problems when individuals aim to maintain or strengthen beliefs in the face of contrary evidence. Poor decisions due to these biases have been made in military, political, and organizational contexts. Cognitive explanations for confirmation bias are based on limitations in people's ability to handle complex tasks and the shortcuts, called "heuristics," that they use.

As this book showed, al-Qaeda sees the world through a particular lens that radicalizes and distorts Islam and that is influenced by the views of extremist thinkers like Sayyid Qutb. Al-Qaeda sees in America what it expects to see through this prism, and it is not likely to change its views—its leaders are not seeking to be educated, and their views are so hardwired that it would take herculean efforts to change them. But although al-Qaeda is a special case, confirmation biases pose a challenge for all individuals at some level.

Confirmation biases are often described as a result of automatic processing that takes place more or less unintentionally. According to Robert Maccoun, evidence that is processed through such bias occurs through a combination of both "hot" (i.e., motivated) and "cold" (i.e., cognitive) mechanisms.[45] Insofar as the bias is unintentional, debiasing approaches can only achieve so much. But more formal procedures for decision making can help, because they indirectly address the bias by pushing decision makers to consider information and options that they might otherwise dismiss from the start. Of course, they may still seek to confirm their original option even if new options are on the table, but at least they will have to confront a comparison among options and a wider set of inputs that may alter how they see a situation.

Another challenge is that confirmation bias serves individual needs. According to social psychologists, people display two tendencies in how they seek or interpret information about themselves. Self-verification aims to bolster the existing self-image, while self-enhancement seeks positive feedback. Both are served by confirmation biases. Experiments show that when people receive feedback that conflicts with their self-image, they are less likely to accept or remember it than when receiving self-verifying feedback, and that they prefer positive feedback—and the people who give it—over negative feedback.[46] Insofar as these findings are instructive, decision makers may try to be more aware of how what they want to hear and what makes them feel better about themselves shape their perceptions. It certainly can't hurt to ask if such dynamics are in play. Do we perceive reality this way because we want to and because it bolsters our self-image? Is negative feedback rejected because it is cognitively comfortable?

By contrast, several steps can help stem confirmation bias in individuals who are open to improving their decision making. Some evidence suggests that strategies to "consider the opposite" or to "consider an alternative" can diminish confirmation bias. In some studies, researchers instructed participants to generate rival points of view or to imagine counterfactual outcomes for a set of events, which is similar to teaching how to consider multiple angles on an issue. Asking others to describe their perceptions of a case is important because it can control for confirmation bias, unless the whole group is subject to similar socialization or group dynamics. In those situations, bringing in outsiders can be vital. Following the rational process can help achieve this goal, as can actively asking others to offer competing views and even appointing a devil's advocate. Certainly, such bias is more likely to stand if groupthink dynamics are in play, so one should be aware of failing to question the leader and should challenge his assumptions.

Analysts should consider how their assumptions shape their views and interpretation of the evidence. Confirmation bias may result when analysts or laypeople think that they know how others think, or how other ethnic or national groups behave. Especially critical are assumptions about what is in another country's national interest and how things are usually done in that country. Assumptions are fine, and cultural analysis depends on them, but we should be careful about the slippery slope to cultural overgeneralization and at least be aware of that potential tendency. Still, as I have noted, other researchers have found that delayed decision making decreases confirmation bias and may permit better evaluation of alternative viewpoints.[47]

On another tack, people expect events to look patterned, and random events to look random, but this is not the case. Random events often look patterned. Because of a need to impose order on their environment, individuals seek and often believe they have found causes for what are actually random phenomena. As discussed earlier, the clustering illusion is the tendency to see nonrandom sequences in a string of random data. Since this illusion may contribute to overconfidence, it may be possible to use debiasing approaches for overconfidence. Mathematical tools or logic could also help, though such approaches have not been tested clearly.

Qualitative approaches may be useful, as well. In my book *The Absence of Grand Strategy*, I noted that it was easy to assume that the most powerful nations pursue and employ consistent, cohesive, and decisive policies in promoting their interests around the world. I discussed how international relations theory emphasizes two grand strategies that great powers may pursue: balance of power policy or hegemonic domination. Yet the evidence in my book showed that such assumptions about how great powers behave are misleading; that, in analyzing U.S. foreign policy in the Persian Gulf from 1972 to 2005, what became clear was that America had no real strategy, that randomness paraded as design, and that U.S. behavior often reflected a lack of careful preparation, inconsistency (even in key beliefs), and reactivity in lieu of grand designs. Studies of this kind, as well as mathematical works and those of logic, can reveal when the clustering illusion—or thinking that sees design where it does not really exist—are in play.

## Thinking Longer Term When Sensible

Longer-term thinking is hard to accomplish because it is difficult to predict how present actions will play out. The future is an abstraction that seems to be neither clear nor especially important compared to the present. Even if we could think long term, what should we think *about* it? What plans should we make?

Some things clearly require long-term planning. The interesting challenge is to get leaders who can identify those things and then think about them in the longer term. Doing so can help, but major hurdles remain: what can we do to get people to accept short-term costs for longer-run benefits? Well, we do this all the time: think of starting an exercise program or cutting out junk food. People suffer short-term pain for longer-run benefits knowing that the end result is beneficial. They know that regular exercise can improve health. They understand how baby steps will add up. The issue is magnified at the complex, political level. How do individuals know that their actions will contribute to the good of the whole, when it depends on others doing the same? Who will deliver the sticks and carrots? How so? How much? What if others cheat by ignoring the law, or by trying to undermine legislation?

Long-term action can be stoked with some simple but rather vital measures. These measures are vital because, as discussed earlier in the book, cognitive psychology experiments have shown that loss is more painful than comparable gain is pleasant, and because people prefer an immediate, smaller gain over taking a chance on a larger, longer-term reward.[48] People across cultures and situations systematically overvalue losses relative to comparable gains.

In the area of oil dependence, longer-term thinking can surely help. But we can't just wave a wand and get leaders and citizens to think in those terms. They need incentives to change short-term thinking into considering longer-term perspectives. One simple measure that can at least help alter these dynamics is nudging. One study has shown, for example, that children are much more likely to eat apples if they have an Elmo sticker on them.[49] Taking a small action like placing a sticker on an apple can nudge children to eat a little healthier. Especially when debiasing is difficult, nudging can be useful to change the environment and choices so as to point people in the right decision. Richard Thaler and Cass Sunstein discuss this at length in their book *Nudge*.[50] It calls upon those who design situations in which choices are made (whether they be the decision makers or other "choice architects") to maximize the odds that decision makers will make wise choices given known decision biases. Making 401(k) enrollment a default, for instance, has been shown to significantly increase employees' savings rates.[51] Kahneman further supports nudging through government policies and institutions, in an informed and unobtrusive way, using behavioral theory (including framing outcomes in terms of losses versus gains) and framing an individual's decisions or "choice" architecture.[52] Perhaps decision makers can even be nudged to institute systematic decision-making procedures that make a rational process more likely.

With regard to energy consumption, we can nudge people to act for the longer term by incentivizing or framing their actions. We can offer incentives to conserve and to reduce pollution. And we can educate them about the longer-run costs, so that at least they understand the possible implications of their behavior. Many economists support raising the federal gasoline tax because they understand that it can create this effect—that higher oil prices can induce efficiency on the part of governments, businesses, and individuals. High prices for fossil fuels—coal, oil, natural gas—help spur development of alternative energy resources as solar, wind, geothermal power generation to become cost-competitive with traditional fossil fuel–fired power plants. Higher prices also encourage conservation by prompting people to use less energy, to establish bike lanes, to build light rail and high-speed rail, to drive more efficient cars, and to use natural gas instead of coal. The higher energy prices go, the more entrepreneurs around the world will embrace alternatives and the more people will conserve.

Yet, as discussed in chapter 5, it was not just individual bias that contributed to short-term thinking, but an array of political and other factors that were not influenced much by emotional stress. Politicians are not reluctant to embrace long-term energy solutions like a carbon tax because of stress. They want to be re-elected. Similarly, consumers buy less efficient vehicles for reasons of price or comfort, while those who purchase hybrids seek to benefit the planet and conceive of themselves as doing just that. Dealing with short-term bias is complicated but may be eased by knowing that it is at work and by understanding how it generates negative effects over time, as in the case of U.S. energy policy. Whatever one thinks of it, there is broad agreement that we have been talking about a serious energy policy for decades and have made only modest progress over that time period.

The question of when short-term thinking arises and represents a cognitive bias with potentially negative implications is not simple to answer. There are temporal trade-offs that must be considered, as well as the context of the decision. For example, short-term thinking may arise more often under conditions of emotional stress, such as when people seek immediate gain[53] and when, due to cognitive limitations, they are more likely to think in local, personal terms rather than global, collective ones.[54]

As the case in this book argued, the status quo bias is related to short-term thinking. It played a role in discussion of U.S. energy policy, and reflects a tendency to stick with what we already have, even when information suggests that change makes sense. There are often good reasons for preferring alternatives that perpetuate the status quo. But studies show that people overvalue the status quo. Barry Schwartz, professor of psychology, suggests that when we make quick decisions, we usually pursue the easiest choice; taking more time can yield a better alternative and can also narrow the field of choices because too many alternatives can be confusing.[55] Economist Niels van de Ven found that delaying a decision for a few days lets us consider that decision when we're well rested and in a different mood. According to his research at the Tilburg Institute for Behavioral Economics Research in the Netherlands, subjects chose the default option eighty-two percent of the time when asked to decide immediately, but only fifty-six percent of the time after some delay.[56] Some evidence also suggests that people estimate that their reactions to future events will be more intense than they actually are.[57] It would be interesting to see if this reinforces the status quo bias by making people less likely to change and, if so, if efforts to change how people see future stakes might help.

## Choose Good Leaders

There is no substitute for experienced and knowledgeable leaders, especially in foreign policy where the stakes are high. Good leaders can help avoid a plethora of errors, including those arising from some cognitive biases. There is no road map for how to choose leaders and assistant leaders at all levels of an organization or government, but the leaders we choose may decrease cognitive biases, as some people are better at making decisions and managing groups than others. Debiasing may be difficult, but preventive measures of this kind, insofar as we can identify leadership skills, can diminish cognitive biases.

Consider the two Bush presidents. The elder Bush was one of the most experienced presidents in the area of foreign policy; his son was one of the least experienced. The first Bush's personal relations proved vital in the Gulf crisis. He knew dozens of world leaders before they took power, and he had immense knowledge of world politics and especially the Middle East through his position as CIA director, U.S. ambassador to the UN, and vice president. His advisers repeatedly emphasized how crucial his role and experience were in the Gulf War, and despite aspects of groupthink dynamics in his administration, he guided the crisis to a successful outcome.[58]

In addition to being less experienced, the younger Bush was far more ideological than his father. He was driven in part by a religious sense and by a perception of American exceptionalism. Neither factor figured much in his father's decision making, perhaps because he relied on his nearly unparalleled foreign policy experience, whereas the son needed cognitive shortcuts. Of course, the differences in decision-making styles relate to how each president lived his life. George W. Bush found God; George H. W. Bush seems to have never lost Him.

It is no accident that the elder Bush avoided the mistakes that his son would go on to make. He and his advisers were much less confident about invading Iraq successfully, and they did not they think they had the mandate from the UN or the American public to do so. By contrast, George W. Bush was far more confident—and, as I tried to show, overconfident—about what could be accomplished in Iraq. Many factors surely contributed to the different approaches of these two presidents, but knowledge and experience in foreign policy, as well as personality style, appears to have been central.

We can't pick leaders based solely on how they make decisions—on their potential to avoid cognitive errors—but we can pay closer attention to their decision-making styles, expertise, and experience. Leaders who are more inclined to initiate rational processes of decision making and to offset possible errors with greater knowledge and experience deserve greater consideration at all levels of decision making—be it local, regional, or global. But experience and knowledge are not important only at the top of a decision-making chain. Decision-making groups should bear that in mind when they pick their leaders, as should all citizens. It's also useful to ensure that subcommittees or groups choose individuals to lead who are most experienced and successful in that area.

## Healthy Group Dynamics

Some scholars think that making decisions in a group setting can help address various biases because, to borrow an old adage, many heads are better than one. Decreasing decision errors has been achieved by having groups rather than individuals make decisions,[59] but whether groups are better than individuals depends on various factors.

Even within a group, the leader matters, because she can direct the entire group. Within the group, dynamics matter, too. Group dynamics are influenced by the group leader but also have a life of their own. Groupthink is a tendency toward agreement, which develops particularly at an early stage of decision making. As I showed in *Explaining Foreign Policy*, aspects of groupthink existed in the Bush administration during the 1990–91 Persian Gulf crisis. In groupthink, "the members' striving for unanimity override their motivation to realistically appraise alternative courses of action."[60] As Irving Janis points out, when "groupthink dominates, suppression of deviant thoughts takes the form of each person's deciding that his misgivings are not relevant, that the benefit of any doubt should be given to the group consensus."[61] As a result, individuals hesitate to dissent, and conflict avoidance becomes a norm.

But while aspects of groupthink did apparently exist in the Gulf crisis, the outcome was not a fiasco. The Gulf War reached a satisfactory conclusion because the leader of the group, President Bush, was experienced and knowledgeable in the subject matter.[62] It follows that if groupthink dynamics are combined with poor leadership, the outcome is likely to be negative.

It is also vital, even in the absence of groupthink, for individuals to develop their own hypotheses, judgments, and estimates independently before working in a group, and then to share ideas with the group in a way that can spark new insights.[63] Any group should be receptive to going through an open-minded process of looking at the options for dealing with problems. If this is not possible because one person in the group takes the lead and exercises power, then the others should try to question the leader or the process. If necessary, it might be useful to find one or more allies that can join in this type of questioning. A few good questions might help, and we shouldn't be shy to ask them for fear of thinking that they don't make sense or that they could get us in trouble.

The way groups discuss information also matters. Many would argue that groups typically possess an informational advantage over individuals, enabling diverse personal experiences, cultural viewpoints, areas of specialization, and educational backgrounds to bring forth a rich pool of information on which to base decision alternatives and relevant criteria. But current findings confirm that although sharing information is important to team outcomes, teams fail to share information when it is most needed.[64] Results from an analysis of seventy-two independent studies of 4,795 groups demonstrate the importance of information sharing to team performance, cohesion, decision satisfaction, and knowledge integration. Three factors affecting team information processing were found to particularly enhance team information sharing: task demonstrability, discussion structure, and cooperation. As one might guess, greater openness influences performance indirectly through promoting high-quality interactions and higher trust in other's informational inputs—something missing in the groupthink dynamic. Openness may also permit more in-depth information processing, thus enhancing the quality of team decisions and yielding unique information.[65]

## Use Analogies Carefully

Analogies can complement or undermine rational approaches. As Philip Tetlock and Charles McGuire argue, "reliance on prior beliefs and expectations becomes irrational only when perseverance and denial dominate openness and flexibility."[66] Analogical thinking can complement rational approaches by helping define the nature of the situation, assess the stakes, provide prescriptions, and evaluate the moral rightness and potential dangers associated with various options.[67] Analogical reasoning appears to offer hope for seeing important, generalizable principles as opposed to getting stuck in details, and for increasing people's awareness.[68] However, analogical thinking can undermine rational processes if it introduces significant biases, excludes or restricts the search for novel information,[69] or pushes actors to ignore facts and options that clash with the message encoded in the analogy,[70] making them less likely or able to consider alternatives.

There's also a danger in assuming that an analogy is suitable, or that conditions are similar to the past when they are not. It is useful to try to compare the current case against the analogy in order to assess similarities and differences—

which sounds so easy but often isn't. It is much easier and quicker to assume that things are the same and to analogize. After all, that is what cognitive shortcuts allow us to do.

## Don't Assume You Understand Others

As Kahneman and Renshon point it, the fundamental attribution error is one of the most common cognitive failures in conflict situations. Even if we know for sure that context, and not a person's characteristics, drive their behavior, we still tend to overattribute behavior to their disposition and personal characteristics—a tendency that is amplified when we are unsure of what has caused their behavior.

This error may be based on an individual's perspective. When we focus on the behavior of others, the person is the primary reference point because we might have little information about their situation. When we focus on our own behavior, we are more aware of what external forces may be influencing us because we know the details of our own situation. Our explanations for other people's behavior are more likely to focus on the person instead of on possible situational forces that may be influencing their behavior.

Several debiasing approaches may reduce the attribution error. Decision makers can ask how they would behave in the same situation and use this thought experiment for better self-exploration; they can also look for unseen causes and focus on factors that they otherwise may ignore, reflect on how they might have contributed to the problem, and present the situation to others and assess how they see it.[71] While preventing attribution errors is difficult, Tetlock found that social accountability can help. Subjects were asked to attribute the behavior of "targets" that had supposedly written pro– or anti–affirmative action essays under conditions of high or low choice. Participants who were told beforehand that they would be held accountable for their explanations of behavior were much less likely to commit attribution errors by emphasizing dispositional influences in the low-choice conditions.[72]

Another debiasing approach comes from game theory. Hayward Alker conducted a series of asymmetric prisoners' dilemma games in which he tracked players' strategies and understandings of their opponents' choices. After time, an interesting phenomenon emerged: the shared understanding of moves changed. In the beginning, defections were treated as indicative of aggressive intent, but later on in the game they were more often considered "mistakes." Alker attributed this to the change in the social context that occurred after the string of mostly cooperative moves by both players.[73]

## Don't Assume Others Understand You

We might assume that if we are virtuous, others will know that, but such thinking is faulty. We must first understand that bias and then question our assumptions about how others see us. Consultation with others, such as outside experts for decision makers, is especially salient as a means of avoiding biased dynamics, which factors like groupthink dynamics, conformity, and decisions shaped by organizational culture may accentuate. In foreign policy, such efforts are especially important because analysts need to try to understand how others think around the world. And as the illusion of transparency suggests, individuals sometimes assume that others know what they are thinking and feeling. Culture gaps make these assumptions even more dangerous. Foreign leaders don't necessarily think like American leaders do, nor do they always understand our message. Understanding the motivations of others may be helpful in assessing to what extent they see us like we see ourselves. It is not safe to assume that the leaders of other countries will do what we would if in their shoes.

It is worth noting studies on the illusion of transparency. In 2003, Kenneth Savitsky and Thomas Gilovich conducted a study to assess whether they could lessen the illusion of transparency. They had participants give impromptu public speeches and then asked them to rate how nervous they thought they appeared to the audience. Most thought they looked like a wreck, but the audience didn't notice it, which in turn made them even more nervous. In a rerun of the experiment, they explained the illusion of transparency to some of the subjects, telling them that the audience did not notice their nervousness. Those told that the audience did not notice their nervousness felt less stressed, gave better speeches, and were viewed as more composed by the audiences.[74] What this might suggest is that we can train people to understand at least a little better that others can't perceive them as well as they perceive themselves.

## Focus Feature

In the case of Iran-Contra, President Reagan emphasized the release of the hostages as a critical variable. It is difficult to question a president's motives, but different approaches to making decisions—using a devil's advocate, for example—might have altered how Reagan weighed the importance of the hostages relative to other goals.

Some of the other rational decision-making procedures discussed earlier in this chapter might also check a tendency to overvalue one variable in a noncompensatory way. Going further, attaching values to different variables may make it more clear that one is focusing heavily on one variable. In cases where this focus is subconscious, it could also be useful to ask decision makers to analyze why they think one variable is so critical and how that is affecting their judgments. Of course, a devil's advocate would also benefit this approach by highlighting other variables that are important.

## Computers, Graphics, and Neuroscience

Some scholars put faith in computers and graphics to help with decision making. Computing technology has improved our ability to calculate and remember. Ward Edwards and Barbara Fasolo speculate that computer-based "decision tools will be as important in the 21st century as spreadsheets were in the 20th century."[75] Silverman investigated whether computers can interact with subjects through modeling and detect their confirmation biases during a problem-solving task. He wanted to know whether computers could decrease the confirmation bias by offering criticism in response to the subject's use of the confirmation bias. The results of his work suggest that computers likely can, although the improvement is sensitive to the strategy used.[76]

In another experiment, graphics helped participants systematically prioritize the most supportive evidence as being most important evidence. The heightened availability of the visually depicted evidence distribution in the graphical versus text format reduced bias. Graphical layout, as compared with text, led participants to choose evidence that was significantly more representative of the balanced evidence pool, an important finding because analysts currently get most of their intelligence in text format. The bias reduction for the graphical layout was attributable to evidence format and not to leading by instruction. We presume that the graphical format helped because it played to the recognition-centered nature of decision making by making the full distribution of evidence constantly available and easy to access.[77]

Cognitive neuroscience can help answer one of the critical questions in political science and international relations: under what conditions do emotions help explain decision making? The tools of cognitive neuroscience have been applied only recently to understanding foreign policy decision making. This work has largely focused on the effect of emotions on decision making, judgment, and learning as well as on how domestic and international events provide feedback, which in turn can influence the decisions of leaders. Myriad other factors may also predict the efficacy of debiasing efforts, including differences in personality and cognitive styles.[78]

## Conclusion

Caveats are in order regarding how to debias and how to enhance decision making. Even the best debiasing efforts face obstacles, some quite serious. For instance, people may be unreceptive to debiasing efforts if they do not consider themselves biased, or if debiasing does not appear to have any real-world value.[79] In addition, one must grapple with the extent to which biases undermine rationality. Are they so prominent that they make a farce out of rationality? Or do they just force us to adjust our views of it?

Cognitive biases also express themselves differently depending on the condition. For instance, sometimes we amplify minor threats and other times underestimate or overlook them. Adolf Hitler and the Munich analogy come to mind. Too many people underestimated Hitler's threat. This example raises an interesting question: if cognitive biases are not always in play, then under what conditions are they most operative?

Debiasing is tricky also because some cognitive biases can have positive effects in smaller doses. Overconfidence can be useful for motivation, so long as it is not too excessive. Underconfidence can stultify progress, immobilize us in the face of opportunities, and incline us to take the easy way out when harder work could have paid off. Similarly, optimism may turn into overoptimism and cloud our judgment, or it can help us get through difficult times that otherwise would have stunted our growth or made us unable to see what was possible. Aristotle said it best: we must have the disposition to choose the mean relative to the extremes, otherwise known as the golden mean. But that is easier said than done. How do we strike that mean? When is too much confidence a bad thing? And can we calibrate debiasing techniques to try to achieve that mean when debiasing is an inexact approach at best?

All these issues are worth pointing out, but it is perhaps enough to know for our purposes here that cognitive biases are important, contribute to bad decisions, and are worth checking if we can. Being aware of cognitive biases and their impact on decision making is critical to us as individuals making our own life decisions, to citizens affected by the decisions of our leaders, and to leaders whose choices have shaped the past, drive the present, and may alter the future. And even if one doubts that we can change these biases by much, it is still vital to understand their role in affecting decisions, because biases are ubiquitous and embedded in our personal and political relations and dynamics. Failing to understand them risks leaving us with blind spots about the human condition—and about the world in which we live.

This glossary lists the cognitive biases discussed in this book and supported by academic study, especially as they relate to foreign policy decision making. While far from exhaustive, it should offer decision makers of all stripes—particularly those in the foreign policy realm—a sense of the field.

## Decision-Making, Belief, and Behavioral Biases

**anchoring.** Overweighting initial impressions, pieces of information, or values. Once set, the anchor of first information learned about an issue can affect future decision making.

**availability heuristic.** Overestimating the likelihood of events that are more available in our memory, which can be influenced by how recent, unusual, or emotionally charged those memories are.

**base rate fallacy.** Basing judgments on specifics while ignoring general statistical information.

**clustering illusion.** Perceiving false "clusters" or "streaks." Clustering illusion results from underestimating how much variability may exist owing to small samples of random or semirandom data.

**confirmation bias.** A bias toward searching for or interpreting information that confirms our conscious and unconscious expectations and worldview.

**focusing illusion.** Overemphasizing the importance of one aspect of an event, causing an error in effectively predicting the value of a future outcome, applied initially to happiness. It suggests that when individuals consider a major life event, such as receiving a big raise, they tend to believe that it will bring more happiness than is the case.

**illusion of control.** Overestimating one's influence over outcomes that may well be determined by chance factors.

**loss aversion.** The notion that the displeasure associated with losing a sum of money is worse than the pleasure of gaining an equivalent sum, meaning that losses are "felt" more than gains. Prospect theory generally describes decision makers who do not systematically seek out the value-maximizing alternative. Loss aversion is a key part of prospect theory, suggesting that decision makers will take greater risks during difficult times and will be risk averse when things are going well.

**noncompensatory decision making.** The notion that foreign policy decisions are often grounded in the rejection or adoption of alternatives on the basis of one or two factors. So much emphasis is placed on one factor that other positive factors cannot compensate for its absence.

**overconfidence.** A condition where subjective confidence in one's judgments is reliably greater than one's objective accuracy; in particular, overestimating the accuracy of one's views, actual capability, and chances of success.

**planning fallacy.** Underestimating the costs, completion times, and risks of planned actions while overestimating the benefits of the same actions.

**short-term thinking.** Privileging short-term considerations over longer-term ones. Studies show that people favor rewards received sooner rather than later; however, their preferences differ in situations where they must choose between smaller immediate and larger delayed rewards.

**status quo bias.** An exaggerated tendency to prefer the status quo over other alternatives.

## Social Biases

**fundamental attribution error.** The overattribution of behavioral characteristics to personal disposition over context. This tendency is amplified when we are unsure of what has caused the behavior.

**groupthink bias.** A tendency to agree, which develops particularly at an early decision-making stage. Group members strive for unanimity and as a result do not appraise alternative options realistically, and even suppress their objections and hesitate to dissent.

**illusion of transparency.** The overestimation of others' ability to understand us, and a reciprocal overestimation of the ability to know others. Individuals often believe their internal states are more apparent to others than is actually the case.

**self-serving bias.** The tendency to claim more responsibility for successes than failures. Self-serving bias may also manifest itself as a tendency to evaluate ambiguous information in a way that is beneficial to self-interests.

## Memory Errors and Biases

**analogical thinking.** Seeking shortcuts to decision making by relying on analogies to past events, which may inform or challenge rational decision making, depending on how they are used.

**illusory correlation.** Relating two unrelated events, such as when people assume that because two events occurred together means that one caused the other.

### Abbreviations

| | |
|---|---|
| CIA | U.S. Central Intelligence Agency |
| CRS | Congressional Research Service |
| FBIS | Foreign Broadcast Information Service |
| GDP | gross domestic product |
| NESA | Near East and South Asia |
| NIC | National Intelligence Council |
| NIE | National Intelligence Estimate |
| NSA | National Security Archives, Washington, D.C. |
| NSDD | National Security Decision Directive |

### Introduction · When Psychology Meets Decision Making

1. I use "decision making" to refer to two things: process and choice. "Process" in this book refers to the nature, content, and origin of our beliefs, perceptions, and preferences and to the objectives of actors. It is what happens in decision making prior to choosing among options. This book is focused mainly at that level.

2. Baron, *Thinking and Deciding*, 61–63. Economists' models assume that people, much like computers, actually tend to make the right choice among the options. Even if we get it wrong, "market forces" set us on the right course. See Ariely, *Predictably Irrational*.

3. Encapsulated in the realist paradigm of international relations. See Freyberg-Inan, Harrison, and James, *Rethinking Realism in International Relations*.

4. Volumes have been written on the value of rational choice, both in terms of its own merits and in comparison to other approaches. See, for instance, Green and Shapiro, *Pathologies of Rational Choice Theory*.

5. See Kahneman, Slovic, and Tversky, *Judgment under Uncertainty*. Unlike rational choice models, which tend to assume that individual differences emerge from differing preference orderings, political psychology explains behavior by delving into the minds of individuals. See Hudson, "Foreign Policy Analysis."

6. Lilienfeld, Ammirati, and Landfield, *Giving Debiasing Away*, 390.

7. Tversky and Kahneman, "Judgment under Uncertainty," 185.

8. Cognitive biases should be distinguished from other forms of bias and from human

emotion. Human emotion can distort decision making, but its study is beyond the scope of this book, except for where emotion and cognitive biases intertwine. Historical analogies in decision making may predispose a person to a cognitive bias of trying to avoid the past, even if the present situation is different, which can trigger an emotional response in an anxious leader. See McDermott, "Feeling of Rationality."

9. See Mintz, "Foreign Policy Decision Making," 2.

10. In a number of seminal experiments, Kahneman and Tversky demonstrated as much. See Kahneman, Slovic, and Tversky, *Judgment under Uncertainty*.

11. Jervis, *Perception and Misperception*, 143.

12. Yetiv, *Explaining Foreign Policy*.

13. Jervis, *Perception and Misperception*. For more comprehensive reviews of work up until the 1990s, see Singer and Hudson, *Political Psychology and Foreign Policy* and Goldgeier and Tetlock, "Psychology and International Relations Theory." See also Mintz and DeRouen, *Understanding Foreign Policy Decision Making*, who include one chapter on biases in decision making.

14. See, for instance, Farnham, "Roosevelt and the Munich Crisis"; Johnson, *Overconfidence and War*; Levy, "Prospect Theory, Rational Choice, and International Relations."

15. Milkman, Chugh, and Bazerman, "How Can Decision Making Be Improved?"

16. See Jervis, *Perception and Misperception*; McDermott, *Political Psychology in International Relations*; McDermott, Wernimont, and Koopman, "Applying Psychology to International Studies"; Welch, *Painful Choices*.

17. For one exception, see Kida, *Don't Believe Everything You Think*.

18. Sanna and Schwarz, "Integrating Temporal Biases."

19. On limitations of the political psychology approach, see Levy, "Political Psychology and Foreign Policy."

20. For an excellent discussion of the costs and benefits of experiments, see McDermott, "Experimental Methods in Political Science."

21. Ariely, *Predictably Irrational*, xxi.

### Chapter 1 · *Afghanistan and Conflict*

1. Lesch, *1979*.

2. On how actors are disinclined to make adequate inferential allowances for their uncertainty about situations, see Griffin, Dunning, and Ross, "Role of Construal Processes in Overconfident Predictions about the Self and Others."

3. On how actors tend to hold unwarrantedly positive views of their own attributes, see Nisbett and Ross, *Human Inference*, 235.

4. Kahneman and Renshon, "Why Hawks Win."

5. Quoted in Ibid., 37.

6. Ibid., 36–37.

7. Quoted in Jervis, *Perception and Misperception in International Politics*, 69.

8. Lebow, "Deterrence," 45.

9. White, *Fearful Warriors*, 177.

10. Savitsky and Gilovich, "Illusion of Transparency."

11. Kahneman and Renshon, "Why Hawks Win," 34–38.

12. Silverstein, "Enemy Images." On threat perception and inflation, see Thrall and Cramer, *American Foreign Policy and the Politics of Fear*.

13. Herrmann and Fischerkeller, "Beyond the Enemy Image and Spiral Model."

14. On factors that shape threat perception, see Jervis, *Perception and Misperception*; Stein, "Building Politics into Psychology." See also McDermott, *Political Psychology in International Politics*; McDermott, Wernimont, and Koopman, "Applying Psychology to International Studies."

15. Herrmann and Fischerkeller, "Beyond the Enemy Image and Spiral Model," 450.

16. Dobrynin, *In Confidence*, 441.

17. For extensive evidence, see Cordovez and Harrison, *Out of Afghanistan*, chap. 1.

18. Gromyko, *Memoirs*, 240.

19. Dobrynin, *In Confidence*, 436.

20. Ibid., 438.

21. James G. Hershberg, ed., "Meeting of the CC CPSU Politburo, 27 April 1978." *Cold War International History Project Bulletin* 8/9 (1996): 112–13.

22. See Cordovez and Harrison, *Out of Afghanistan*, chap. 1., esp. 36–37.

23. Cited in Bradsher, "Soviet Union and the War in Afghanistan," 132.

24. Dobrynin, *In Confidence*, 438.

25. Cordovez and Harrison, *Out of Afghanistan*, 45.

26. Cited in Dobrynin, *In Confidence*, 440. For a good, concise discussion of the defensive motives of the invasion, see Bradsher, "Soviet Union and the War in Afghanistan," 130–33.

27. Herrmann and Fischerkeller, "Beyond the Enemy Image and Spiral Model," 449–50.

28. Vance, *Hard Choices*, 391.

29. See, for instance, the statement by former Under Secretary of State for Security Assistance Matthew Nimitz, "U.S. Security Framework," 1–4.

30. Even *Izvestia*, the official Soviet government newspaper, recognized that the invasion gave U.S. hardliners a boost. Bradsher, *Afghanistan and the Soviet Union*, 191.

31. Ibid., 47.

32. Citing his own testimony, Vance, *Hard Choices*, 396.

33. Westad, *Global Cold War*, 322.

34. Ibid., 17.

35. Quoted in Halliday, *Soviet Policy in the Arc of Crisis*, 9.

36. Carter, *Public Papers*, 2236.

37. Jimmy Carter, interview by Bill Monroe, Carl T. Rowan, David Broder, and Judy Woodruff, *Meet the Press*, NBC, January 20, 1980.

38. "Transcript of President's State of the Union Address to Joint Session of Congress," *New York Times*, January 24, 1980, A12.

39. Jimmy Carter, interview on *Meet the Press*, January 20, 1980.

40. Carter, *Keeping Faith*, 472. Based on documents from the Carter Presidential Library, one scholar argues that Carter exaggerated the threat of the Soviet invasion of Afghanistan, and grossly overreacted. Kaufman, *Presidency of James Earl Carter, Jr.*

41. Carter, *Keeping Faith*, 471.

42. Jimmy Carter, "The State of the Union Address Delivered before a Joint Session of the Congress," January 23, 1980.

43. See "Soviet Buildup near Iran Tested Carter," *New York Times*, August 27, 1986, A3.

44. Yetiv, *America and the Persian Gulf*.

45. Harold Brown, interview, *Wall Street Journal*, July 1, 1980, 22.

46. See U.S. Senate, *First Concurrent Resolution on the Budget, Fiscal Year 1981* (Washington, DC: Congressional Budget Office, 1981), 384.

47. See U.S. Congress, *Rapid Deployment Forces: Policy and Budgetary Implications* (Washington, DC: Congressional Budget Office, 1983), XIV, 4, 8, 11.

48. Reagan, *Public Papers*, 873, 952.

49. Ronald Reagan, "Remarks at the Annual Convention of the National Association of Evangelicals in Orlando, Florida," March 8, 1983.

50. For instance, Hurwitz, Peffley, and Seligson, "Foreign Policy Belief Systems in Comparative Perspective."

51. Rashid, *Taliban*, 18.

52. Brisard and Martinez, *Zarqawi*, 25. See also Johnson, "Financing Afghan Terrorism," 109–11.

53. Scheuer, *Through Our Enemies' Eyes*, 100–105.

54. United States v. Osama bin Laden, No. S(7) 98 Cr. 1023 (S.D.N.Y. 2001) (Court Testimony of al-Qaeda Operative Jamal al-Fadl), 218–19.

55. On such effects, see Coll, *Ghost Wars*.

56. Wright, *Sacred Rage*, 250, 257.

57. Quoted in Schweitzer and Shay, *Globalization of Terror*, 118.

58. *Osama bin Laden*, No. S(7) 98 Cr. 1023, 218–19.

59. Bradsher, *Afghanistan and the Soviet Union*.

60. Cited in Hammond, *Red Flag over Afghanistan*, 139.

61. Dobrynin, *In Confidence*, 448.

62. "Excerpts from Brezhnev Statement Answering a Question on World Situation," *New York Times*, January 13, 1980, A16.

63. Ibid., 189–204.

64. Dobrynin, *In Confidence*, 439.

65. Ibid., 448, 452.

66. Holland, "Soviet Invasion of Afghanistan," 20.

67. Bureau of Intelligence and Research, "Afghanistan: Soviet Occupation and Withdrawal," *Department of State Bulletin* 89 (March 1989), 72–74.

68. Jervis, "Cooperation under the Security Dilemma."

69. Ibid.

## Chapter 2 · *President Reagan and Iran-Contra*

1. Richard Neustadt, *Presidential Power and the Modern Presidents*, rev. ed. (New York: Free Press, 1991).

2. Brands, "Inside the Iraqi State Records."

3. Anchoring is the tendency to rely too heavily on, or to "anchor," one trait or piece of information when making decisions. Once the anchor is set, the first information learned about a subject can affect future decision making and information analysis.

4. Schkade and Kahneman, "Does Living in California Make People Happy?"; Kahneman et al., "Would You Be Happier If You Were Richer?," 5782.

5. Arana and Leon, "Understanding the Use of Non-Compensatory Decision Rules."

6. Mintz, "How Do Leaders Make Decisions"; Goertz, "Constraints, Compromises, and Decision Making." See also Mintz, "Decision to Attack Iraq"; Yetiv, *Explaining Foreign Policy*.

7. Mintz and Geva, "Poliheuristic Theory of Foreign Policy Decisionmaking," 84–85.

8. For a brief explanation and for the evidence, see Mintz and DeRouen, *Understanding Foreign Policy Decision Making*, 34–37. See also Mintz and Geva, "Poliheuristic Theory of Foreign Policy Decisionmaking," 6–7.

9. U.S. National Security Council, Oliver North Notebook Entries for November 27, 1985, IC-01922, NSA. The United States also requested that Iran quit its support of terrorism.

10. John Poindexter to Ronald W. Reagan, "Covert Action Finding Regarding Iran," January 6, 1983, IC-0201, NSA.

11. See Tower, Muskie, and Scowcroft, *Tower Commission Report*, chap. 4.

12. Ibid., xv.

13. "Rumsfeld Mission: December 20 Meeting with Iraqi President Saddam Hussein," U.S. Department of State cable, January 13, 1994.

14. "U.S. Policy toward Iran," NSDD, NSC/ICS 402010, June 11, 1985, declassified memo to Robert McFarlane.

15. Tower, Muskie, and Scow, *Tower Commission Report*, 20.

16. Powell and Persico, *My American Journey*, 294.

17. Ibid., 294.

18. Caspar W. Weinberger to Robert C. McFarlane, "U.S. Policy toward Iran," IG-00266, July 16, 1985, NSA.

19. Ibid.

20. George P. Shultz to Robert C. McFarlane, "U.S. Policy toward Iran: Comment on Draft, National Security Decision Directive," IG-00261, June 29, 1985, NSA.

21. Powell and Persico, *My American Journey*, 300.

22. U.S. Department of State, Bureau of Near Eastern and South Asian Affairs, "The Gulf War, Secret Briefing Paper," IG-00311, February 27, 1986, NSA.

23. Michael H. Armacost to Office of the Secretary of State, "Arms Sales to Iran," IC-02759, May 3, 1986, NSA.

24. See Cordesman, *Iran–Iraq War and Western Security*, 93–102.

25. U.S. Department of State, Bureau of Near Eastern and South Asian Affairs, "The Gulf War, Secret, Briefing Paper."

26. Armacost to Office of the Secretary of State, "Arms Sales to Iran."

27. Ibid.

28. See Walsh, *Iran-Contra*, 16–24. He was the independent council for the Iran-Contra hearings.

29. Pollack, *Persian Puzzle*, 219.

30. See "U.S. Policy toward Iran," NSDD, NSC/ICS 402010, June 11, 1985. See also "Covert Action Finding Regarding Iran," January 17, 1986, memo to the president from Poindexter.

31. "U.S. Policy toward Iran," NSDD, NSC/ICS 402010, June 11, 1985.

32. "Toward a Policy on Iran," NIC 02545-85, May 17, 1985, declassified memo from Graham Fuller to the director of the CIA.

33. Ibid., 928.

34. See Walsh, *Iran-Contra*, 1–24.

35. Tower, Muskie, and Scowcroft, *Tower Commission Report*, 36. See also Strober and Strober, *Reagan Presidency*, 390.

36. See Walsh, *Iran-Contra*, 277–78.

37. Colin Powell, chairman, Joint Chiefs of Staff, interview with author, Alexandria, Va., May 30, 1996.

38. Strober and Strober, *Reagan Presidency*, 403.

39. Quoted in Pollack, *Persian Puzzle*, 212.

40. Ibid., 212–13.

41. Rothkopf, *Running the World*, 244.

42. Strober and Strober, *Reagan Presidency*, 449.

43. "Diary," NSAEBB 210/14, December 7, 1985, handwritten note by Caspar Weinberger, NSA, http://www.gwu.edu/~nsarchiv/NSAEBB/NSAEBB210/14-Weinberger%20Diaries%20Dec%207%20handwritten.pdf.

44. Reagan, "Address to the Nation on the Iran Arms and Contra Aid Controversy," March 4, 1987, http://www.reagan.utexas.edu/archives/speeches/1987/030487h.htm.

45. Citing Nofziger and discussing beliefs, Jervis, "Understanding Beliefs," 659.

46. Powell, interview with author, May 30, 1996.

47. See Walsh, *Iran-Contra*, 228–29.

48. Powell described Defense Secretary Weinberger in these terms in his interview with the author, May 30, 1996.

49. Tower, Muskie, and Scowcroft, *Tower Commission Report*, 225. See also Walsh, *Iran-Contra*, chaps. 9 and 10. On the vice president's role, see Walsh, *Iran-Contra*, 247–48.

50. For instance, "U.S. Policy toward Iran," NSDD, NSC/ICS 402010, June 11, 1985; "Toward a Policy on Iran," NIC 02545-85, May 17, 1985. See also Walsh, *Iran-Contra*, 1–24, chap. 9.

51. Top secret memo from Robert McFarlane, The White House, June 17, 1985.

52. Strober and Strober, *Reagan Presidency*, 439–40.

53. Walsh, *Iran-Contra*, 193. On the role of high-level administration officials, see also Walsh, *Firewall*.

54. Tower, Muskie, and Scowcroft, *Tower Commission Report*, 28, 36–39, 200–225. See also Walsh, *Iran-Contra Affair*, 277–78.

55. U.S. National Security Council, Oliver North Notebook Entries for November 26, 1985, IC-01909, NSA.

56. Reagan to William J. Casey, "Top Secret Presidential Finding," January 17, 1986, IC-02182, NSA.

57. See Walsh, *Iran-Contra*, 163, 167.

58. Rothkopf, *Running the World*, 246.

59. Ibid., 250.

60. Brands, "Inside the Iraqi State Records."

61. Yetiv, *Explaining Foreign Policy*.

### Chapter 3 · Radical Terrorism

1. See the analysis of a former intelligence officer in Scheuer, *Imperial Hubris*.

2. Ramachandran and Blakelee, *Phantoms in the Brain*.

3. Baron, *Thinking and Deciding*, 162–65.

4. For a review, see McKenzie, "Judgment and Decision Making."

5. See Jones and Sugden, "Positive Confirmation Bias in the Acquisition of Information."

6. Baron, *Thinking and Deciding*, 162–64.

7. Shermer, *Believing Brain*, 5.
8. Ariely, *Predictably Irrational*, 164–72.
9. Shermer, *Believing Brain*, 82.
10. Tetlock, "Accountability and the Perseverance of First Impressions."
11. See Risen and Gilovich, "Informal Logical Fallacies."
12. Duelfer and Dyson, "Chronic Misperception and International Conflict."
13. See Chabris and Simons, *Invisible Gorilla*.
14. Baron, *Thinking and Deciding*, 192–96.
15. Kida, *Don't Believe Everything You Think*, 106–7.
16. See Baron, *Thinking and Deciding*, 199.
17. See Jervis, "Deterrence and Perception."
18. On the impact of images on perception and reaction, see Castano, Sacchi, and Gries, "Perception of the Other in International Relations," http://www.newschool.edu/uploadedFiles/Faculty/NSSR/Castano_PerceptionOfOther.pdf. See also Ibroscheva, "Is There Still an Evil Empire?"
19. On this literature, see Wallace, Suedfeld, and Thachuk, "Political Rhetoric of Leaders under Stress in the Gulf Crisis," 95–96. On the impact of stress, see Janis and Mann, *Decision Making*. See also Brecher, "State Behavior in a Crisis," 446–80.
20. Jervis, *Perception and Misperception*, 291–96.
21. Gilovich, *How We Know What Isn't So*. See also the classic paper on streaks, Vallone and Tversky, "Hot Hand in Basketball."
22. Whitson and Galinksy, "Lacking Control Increases Illusory Pattern Perception," http://rifters.com/real/articles/Science_LackingControlIncreasesIllusoryPatternPerception.pdf.
23. Hastie and Dawes, *Rational Choice in an Uncertain World*, 160.
24. Hood, *SuperSense*.
25. For a more complete examination of erroneous beliefs, see Kahneman, Slovic, and Tversky, *Judgment under Uncertainty*.
26. Langer, "Psychology of Chance."
27. Taleb, *Black Swan*, 8.
28. Taleb, *Fooled by Randomness*.
29. Taleb, *Black Swan*.
30. Lilienfeld et al., "Giving Debiasing Away," 391.
31. This is associated with Salafi Islamic thought. See Moghadam, "Motives for Martyrdom," 62–78. See Wiktorowicz, "New Global Threat"; Fandy, *Saudi Arabia and the Politics of Dissent*, 190–92.
32. This notion may well be shared by Islamists and liberals in Muslim countries. Wedeen, "Beyond the Crusades," 58.
33. CNN, October 8, 2001.
34. Ibrahim, Zawahiri, and bin Laden, *Al-Qaeda Reader*, esp. 20.
35. Juergensmeyer, *Terror in the Mind of God*, 263–78; Stern, *Ultimate Terrorists*.
36. See Fuller, *Future of Political Islam*, chap. 8. For bin Laden, jihad is a holy war against the infidels; in mainstream Islam, jihad means a struggle against oneself for self-improvement.
37. See Qutb, *Milestones*. On the writings of extremists, see Schweitzer and Shay, *Globalization of Terror*, chap. 1. For a brief argument that Qutb has been misunderstood, see Khan, "Radical Islam, Liberal Islam."

38. See Wright, *Looming Tower*, chap. 2.
39. Qutb, *Milestones*.
40. Translated in Laqueur, *Voices of Terror*, 394.
41. See Qutb, *Milestones*, 79, 97, 101–2.
42. For this document and a cogent analysis of it, see Ibrahim, Zawahiri, and bin Laden, *Al-Qaeda Reader*, 66.
43. Murawiec, *Mind of Jihad*, esp. 37.
44. Ibrahim, Zawahiri, and bin Laden, *Al-Qaeda Reader*, 137–74.
45. Hafez, *Why Muslims Rebel*, 99.
46. Ibid., 188.
47. Quoted in Kepel, *Jihad*, 318.
48. Quoted in Bodansky, *Bin Laden*, 11.
49. See Pape, *Dying to Win*, 117–19.
50. See Hussein and Bengio, *Saddam Speaks on the Gulf Crisis*.
51. *New York Times*, September 20, 2002, A12.
52. Yetiv, *Petroleum Triangle*.
53. This section is based on several Osama bin Laden videos shown on CNN during the period September 15 to October 15, 2001.
54. *Baghdad INA*, in FBIS: NESA, October 10, 1990, 27.
55. Pape sees suicide terrorism as a fundamental response to foreign occupation. Pape, *Dying to Win*.
56. *New York Times*, December 27, 2001, B4.
57. See "Bin Laden's Fatwa," PBS, August 23, 1996, www.pbs.org/newshour/terrorism/international/fatwa_1996.html.
58. For more analysis, see Bergen, *Holy War, Inc.*, esp. 95–96.
59. Pape finds that the U.S. military presence in the Middle East accounts for forty-three of sixty-seven (sixty-four percent) of al-Qaeda suicide attacks, including the one from Lebanon. Pape, *Dying to Win*, 114.
60. For more analysis, see Bergen, *Holy War, Inc.*, esp. 95–96.
61. See Karam, *Transnational Political Islam*.
62. See "Arab Public Opinion Surveys," Anwar Sadat Chair for Peace and Development, http://www.sadat.umd.edu/new%20surveys/surveys.htm.
63. See "Global Public Opinion in the Bush Years," Pew Research Global Attitudes Project, http://pewglobal.org/reports/display.php?ReportID=263.
64. See Benjamin and Simon, *Age of Sacred Terror*, 157–58.
65. See transcript in Aust et al., *Inside 9-11*, 316.
66. See Qutb, *Milestones*, esp. chap. 7.
67. For a transcript of the audiotape, see http://news.bbc.co.uk/2/hi/middle_east/3368957.stm.
68. Translated and analyzed in Kepel and Milelli, *Al-Qaeda in Its Own Words*.
69. On the Iraq War, Schweitzer and Ferber, *Al-Qaeda and the Internationalization of Suicide Terrorism*, esp. 80–81.
70. See, for instance, Whitlock, "Commandos Free Hostages Being Held in Saudi Arabia."
71. See Lynch, "Anti-Americanisms in the Arab World," 211.

72. See "Testimony of Andrew Kohut," House Committee on Foreign Affairs, March 4, 2010, http://democrats.foreignaffairs.house.gov/111/koh030410.pdf.

73. Tenet, "Converging Dangers in a Post 9/11 World."

74. Ibid.

75. Perl, "Terrorism, the Future, and U.S. Foreign Policy."

76. For an extensive discussion, see Myers, *Eyes on the Horizon.*

77. Jenkins, *Will Terrorists Go Nuclear?*, 255.

78. Ibid., 256–58.

79. For an extensive discussion, see Scheuer, *Imperial Hubris*, esp. 155–58.

80. See "Testimony of Dr. Steven Kull," House Committee on Foreign Affairs, May 17, 2007.

## Chapter 4 · The 2003 Invasion of Iraq

1. On this voluminous literature, see Johnson, *Overconfidence and War.*

2. Renshon, "Assessing Capabilities in International Politics." For a more nuanced analysis of definitions, see Moore and Healy, "Trouble with Overconfidence."

3. See, for instance, Gigerenzer, *Adaptive Thinking*, 246–48.

4. Bukszar, "Does Overconfidence Lead to Poor Decisions?"

5. See, for example, Renshon, "Assessing Capabilities."

6. See McGraw, Mellers, and Ritov, "Affective Costs of Overconfidence"; Fischhoff, "Debiasing."

7. On this literature, see Moore and Healy, "Trouble with Overconfidence."

8. Ariely, *Upside of Irrationality*; Frey, *Inspiring Economics*, 44–45. On studies of this factor, see Frey and Stutzer, *Happiness and Economics.*

9. Odean, "Volume, Volatility, Price, and Profit"; Barber and Odean, "Boys Will Be Boys."

10. On these studies, see Kida, *Don't Believe Everything You Think*, 140–41.

11. Malkiel, *Random Walk down Wall Street.*

12. Johnson, *Overconfidence and War*, 5–26.

13. This section is based on Kruger and Dunning, "Unskilled and Unaware of It."

14. Psychologists sometimes treat these two phenomena as distinct, but for international relations scholars, they both tie into perceptions of chances of victory—a key aspect of how such scholars see overconfidence.

15. Johnson, *Overconfidence and War.*

16. On failed prediction by experts, see Tetlock, *Expert Political Judgment.*

17. On the hindsight literature, see Hawkins and Hastie, "Hindsight."

18. "President Bush Outlines Iraqi Threat," The White House, October 7, 2002, http://georgewbush-whitehouse.archives.gov/news/releases/2002/10/20021007-8.html.

19. Remarks by President Bush on Iraq in the Rose Garden, September 26, 2002, http://georgewbush-whitehouse.archives.gov/news/releases/2002/09/20020926-7.html.

20. See CIA, "National Intelligence Estimate: Iraq's Continuing Programs for Weapons of Mass Destruction," October 2002, NIE 2002-16HC.

21. Dick Cheney, "The Risks of Inaction Are Far Greater Than the Risk of Action," Address to the 103rd National Convention of the Veterans of Foreign Wars, August 26, 2002.

22. The full text of the January 28, 2003, State of the Union address appears at http://www.gpo.gov/fdsys/pkg/WCPD-2003-02-03/pdf/WCPD-2003-02-03-Pg109.pdf.

23. The full text of the January 29, 2002, State of the Union address appears at http://www.gpo.gov/fdsys/pkg/WCPD-2002-02-04/pdf/WCPD-2002-02-04-Pg133-3.pdf.

24. Remarks by the President and British Prime Minister Tony Blair, The White House, January 31, 2003, http://georgewbush-whitehouse.archives.gov/news/releases/2003/01/20030131-23.html.

25. Remarks by the President on Iraq, Cincinnati, Ohio, October 7, 2002, http://georgewbush-whitehouse.archives.gov/news/releases/2002/10/20021007-8.html.

26. The full text of the memo appears at http://www.downingstreetmemo.com/memos.html.

27. See Kaufmann, "Threat Inflation and the Failure of the Marketplace of Ideas."

28. Testimony by Secretary of Defense Donald H. Rumsfeld to the Senate Armed Services Committee, July 9, 2003, http://www.au.af.mil/au/awc/awcgate/congress/rumsfeld_09july03.pdf.

29. See the account by the former counterterrorism chief in Clarke, *Against All Enemies*, 30.

30. Testimony of national security advisor Condoleezza Rice to the 9/11 Commission, April 8, 2004. On the impact of 9/11, see also Woodward, *Bush at War*, 34–35; "US Decision on Iraq Has Puzzling Past: Opponents of War Wonder When, How Policy Was Set," *Washington Post*, January 12, 2003.

31. Radio Address by the President to the Nation, Office of the Press Secretary, December 7, 2002.

32. "Statement by the President in His Address to the Nation," September 11, 2001.

33. See, for instance, the President's Address to the American Enterprise Institute, February 26, 2003, http://www.guardian.co.uk/world/2003/feb/27/usa.iraq2.

34. Haass, *War of Necessity*.

35. Woodward, *State of Denial*, 120–21.

36. On the substantial failure in planning, see Mitchell and Massoud, "Anatomy of Failure."

37. Whitaker, "Flags in the Dust," http://www.guardian.co.uk/world/2003/mar/24/worlddispatch.iraq.

38. See Pillar, *Intelligence and U.S. Foreign Policy*, 60–61.

39. Gordon and Trainor, *Endgame*, 685.

40. See Bensahel, "Mission Not Accomplished."

41. For useful accounts of this period, see Gordon and Trainor, *Endgame*.

42. Cited in Pillar, *Intelligence and U.S. Foreign Policy*, 59.

43. Bush, *Decision Points*, 256–57.

44. Feith, *War and Decision*, 275.

45. Colin Powell, "The General's Orders," Newsweek, May 21, 2012.

46. Gordon and Trainor, *Endgame*, 15, 29.

47. On his testimony, see http://www.youtube.com/watch?v=a_xchyIeCQw.

48. See Shanker, "New Strategy Vindicates Ex–Army Chief Shinseki," http://www.nytimes.com/2007/01/12/washington/12shinseki.html.

49. "President's Address to the Nation," Office of the Press Secretary, January 10, 2007. http://georgewbush-whitehouse.archives.gov/news/releases/2007/01/20070110-7.html.

50. See Belasco, "Cost of Iraq, Afghanistan, and Other Global War on Terror Operations since 9/11," http://www.fas.org/sgp/crs/natsec/RL33110.pdf.

51. Stigliz and Bilmes, "Three Trillion Dollar War."

52. See Ricks, *Fiasco*. His book is based on hundreds of interviews and more than thirty-seven thousand pages of documents.

53. See Johnson, *Overconfidence and War*, 196–204.

54. On this argument, see Mitchell and Massoud, "Anatomy of Failure."

55. I participated in this 2003 conference.

56. Pillar, *Intelligence and U.S. Foreign Policy*, 51–55.

57. Ibid.

58. Ibid.

59. For a sober assessment, see Pfiffner, "Did President Bush Mislead the Country in His Arguments for War with Iraq?"

60. Pillar, "Intelligence, Policy, and the War in Iraq."

61. On Iraq and nuclear materials from Niger, for instance, see Wilson, *Politics of Truth*, chap. 15.

62. Pillar, "Intelligence, Policy, and the War in Iraq."

63. Haass, *War of Necessity*, 235.

64. Yetiv, *Explaining Foreign Policy*.

65. Scowcroft, "Don't Attack Saddam."

66. On this opposition, see Mann, *Rise of the Vulcans*, 336–41.

67. Clancy, Zinni, and Koltz, *Battle Ready*.

68. "War in Iraq Is *Not* in America's National Interest," *New York Times*, September 26, 2002.

69. Johnson et al., "Overconfidence in War Games."

70. Moore and Healy, "Trouble with Overconfidence."

71. Secretary of State Colin Powell on C-SPAN, December 8, 2004.

72. Bush, *Decision Points*.

73. For a good, brief description of this study, see Rendall and Broughel, "Amplifying Officials, Squelching Dissent."

74. Borjesson, *Feet to the Fire*.

75. Kaufmann, "Threat Inflation."

76. Haass, *War of Necessity*, 235.

77. Ibid., 234.

78. DeYoung, *Soldier*, 429.

79. Woodward, *Plan of Attack*, 416.

80. Tenet, *At the Center of the Storm*, 308.

81. Diamond et al., "Iraq Course Set from Tight White House Circle," http://www.usatoday.com/news/world/2002-09-10-iraq-war_x.htm.

82. Draper, *Dead Certain*.

83. Bacevich and Prodromou, "God Is Not Neutral," 49.

84. Remarks by President Bush upon Arrival at the South Lawn, September 16, 2001, http://georgewbush-whitehouse.archives.gov/news/releases/2001/09/20010916-2.html.

85. Juergensmeyer, "Religious Terror and Global War."

86. See Peters, "Firanj Are Coming—Again."

87. On how entrepreneurs are overconfident and what this causes, see Lowe and Ziedonis, "Overoptimism and the Performance of Entrepreneurial Firms."

88. On these works, see Baron, *Thinking and Deciding*, 216.

89. Montier, *Behavioural Finance.*
90. Buehler, Griffin, and Ross, "Exploring the 'Planning Fallacy.'"
91. Yetiv, *Explaining Foreign Policy.*
92. Ariely, *Predictably Irrational.*

### Chapter 5 · U.S. Energy Policy

1. "National Security Consequences of U.S. Oil Dependence," Independent Task Force Report No. 58, Council on Foreign Relations, 2006, 3.
2. On the various costs of the oil era, see Yetiv, *Petroleum Triangle*; Duffield, *Over a Barrel*; Moran and Russell, *Energy Security and Global Politics*; Klare, *Blood and Oil*; Rutledge, *Addicted to Oil*; Smil, *Energy at the Crossroads*; and Speth, *Red Sky at Morning.* One notable study found that the costs of inaction on climate change would be around five percent of global GDP per year, versus costing one percent of GDP to take action. See discussion in Hakes, *Declaration of Energy Independence*, 115.
3. Juhasz, *Tyranny of Oil.*
4. See Yergin, *Prize*, 615–19.
5. To read this speech and an analysis of what it meant during this time, see Horowitz, *Jimmy Carter and the Energy Crisis of the 1970s*, 33–42.
6. Bill Clinton, "The President's News Conference," The American Presidency Project, June 28, 2000, http://www.presidency.ucsb.edu/ws/index.php?pid=1666.
7. See Hakes, *Declaration of Energy Independence.*
8. "U.S. Oil Import Dependence: Declining No Matter How You Measure It," This Week in Petroleum, May 25, 2011, http://www.eia.gov/oog/info/twip/twiparch/110525/twipprint.html.
9. Speech by President Bush on Energy at the White House, June 18, 2008, http://www.cfr.org/energy/president-bushs-speech-energy-june-2008/p16589.
10. Remarks by President Bush on America's Energy Security at Georgetown University, March 30, 2011, http://www.whitehouse.gov/the-press-office/2011/03/30/remarks-president-americas-energy-security.
11. "Barack Obama on Energy and Oil," On the Issues, http://www.ontheissues.org/2008/barack_obama_energy_+_oil.htm.
12. Miller, "Obama," http://abcnews.go.com/blogs/politics/2011/03/obama-we-cant-hit-the-snooze-button-when-gas-prices-fall-again/.
13. For summaries, see Holt and Glover, "Energy Policy Act of 2005"; Sissine, "Energy Independence and Security Act of 2007."
14. "Costs of Oil Dependence 2008: Fact #522," U.S. Department of Energy Vehicle Technologies Office, June 9, 2008, http://www1.eere.energy.gov/vehiclesandfuels/facts/2008_fotw522.html.
15. President Dwight D. Eisenhower, Farewell Address to the Nation, January 17, 1961, http://www.h-net.org/~hst306/documents/indust.html.
16. On short- versus long-run trade-offs, see Khalil, *New Behavioral Economics.*
17. Heinen and Low, "Human Behavioral Ecology and Environmental Conservation."
18. Milkman, Rogers, and Bazerman, "Harnessing Our Inner Angels and Demons."
19. On this literature, see Manuck et al., "Neurobiology of Intertemporal Choice."
20. Montier, *Behavioural Investing.*
21. See Camerer, Loewenstein, and Prelec, "Neuroeconomics."

22. This paragraph is based on Massari, "Of Two Minds."
23. Manuck et al., "A Neurobiology of Intertemporal Choice," 139–72.
24. Camerer, Loewenstein, and Prelece, "Neuroeconomics," 39–40.
25. Gray, "Bias Toward Short-Term Thinking."
26. Mintz and DeRouen, *Understanding Foreign Policy Decision Making*, 41.
27. See Yetiv and Fowler, "Challenges of Decreasing Oil Consumption."
28. This paragraph is based on calculations in Yetiv and Fowler, "Challenges of Decreasing Oil Consumption."
29. Hakes, *Declaration of Energy Independence*.
30. Chris Isidore, "GM CEO Calls for $1 Gas Tax Hike," CNNMoney, June 7, 2011, money.cnn.com/2011/06/07/news/companies/gm_gas_tax_hike/index.htm.
31. Mankiw, "Gas Tax Now!" See also Mankiw, "Raise the Gas Tax"; Mankiw, "Greenspan on Gas Taxes."
32. See Lydia Saad, "In U.S., Global Warming Views Steady Despite Warmer Winter," March 30, 2012, http://www.gallup.com/poll/153608/global-warming-views-steady-despite-warm-winter.aspx.
33. Sipes and Mendelsohn, "Effectiveness of Gasoline Taxation."
34. Quoted in Hakes, *Declaration of Energy Independence*, 224.
35. "Peak Oil Quotes: Statements by Key Individuals," Oil Depletion Analysis Centre, http://odac-info.org/peak-oil-quotes.
36. "Majority of Americans Oppose Gas Tax, New Energy Taxes in Wake of Oil Spill," Institute for Energy Research, July 7, 2010, http://www.instituteforenergyresearch.org/2010/07/07/poll-majority-of-americans-oppose-gas-tax-new-energy-taxes-in-wake-of-gulf-oil-spill/.
37. See, for example, Berestaanu and Li, "Gasoline Prices, Government Support, and the Demand for Hybrid Vehicles."
38. For a review, see Milkman, Rogers, and Bazerman, "Harnessing Our Inner Angels and Demons."
39. Ibid.
40. On hybrid trends, see "Maps and Data," U.S. Department of Energy Alternative Fuels Data Center, http://www.afdc.energy.gov/afdc/data/vehicles.html#afv_hev.
41. "Consumers Want More Fuel-Efficient Vehicles, but Are Confused about the Options," PR Newswire, July 11, 2011, http://www.prnewswire.com/news-releases/consumers-want-more-fuel-efficient-vehicles-but-are-confused-about-the-options-125367898.html.
42. Steiner, "Consumer Views on Transportation and Energy."
43. Sperling and Cannon, *Reducing Climate Impacts in the Transportation Sector*, 196.
44. Turrentine, Kurani, and Heffner, "Fuel Economy," 18. See also Turrentine, "Car Buyers and Fuel Economy?" On this literature, see Diamond, "Impact of Government Incentives for Hybrid-Electric Vehicles," 973.
45. Kahn, "Do Greens Drive Hummers or Hybrids?"
46. Heffner, Kurani, and Turrentine, "Symbolism in California's Early Market for Hybrid Electric Vehicles."
47. For data, see American Public Transportation Association, *The Case for Business Investment in High-Speed and Intercity Passenger Rail* (Washington, DC, 2012), 4.
48. Paul Krugman, "The Conscience of a Liberal," *New York Times*, August 25, 2009.
49. Sperling and Cannon, *Reducing Climate Impacts in the Transportation Sector*, 114–15.

50. Yafee, "Why Environmental Policy Nightmares Recur."

51. Hardin, "Tragedy of the Commons."

52. On how the problems associated with the commons differ from the problems associated with a pure public good, see Sandler and Arce, "Pure Public Goods versus Commons."

53. Hardin, "Tragedy of the Commons," in Ostrom, *Governing the Commons*; Gardner, and Walker, *Rules, Games, and Common–Pool Resources*.

54. Ostrom, "Coping with Tragedies of the Commons"; Milinski, Semmann and Krambeck, "Reputation Helps Solve the 'Tragedy of the Commons.'"

55. For a good introduction to the literature on status quo bias and related phenomena, see Kahneman and Tversky, *Choices, Values, and Frames*. Bostrom and Ord, "Status Quo Bias in Bioethics."

56. Fernandez and Rodrik, "Resistance to Reform."

57. Bostrom and Ord, "Status Quo Bias in Bioethics."

58. Kahneman, Knetsch, and Thaler, "Anomalies"; Samuelson and Zeckhauser, "Status Quo Bias in Decision Making."

59. Samuelson and Zeckhauser, "Status Quo Bias in Decision Making."

60. Ibid.

61. Kahneman, Knetsch, and Thaler, "Anomalies," 164.

62. On short- versus long-run tradeoffs, see Khalil, *New Behavioral Economics*. Prospect theory can overlap with rational choice models in some ways. See de Mesquita and McDermott, "Crossing No Man's Land."

63. See, for instance, Welch, *Painful Choices*. Levy, "Prospect Theory, Rational Choice, and International Relations."

64. Taliaferro, *Balancing Risks*, 14.

65. Farnham, "Roosevelt and the Munich Crisis."

66. Haas, "Prospect Theory and the Cuban Missile Crisis."

67. Levy, "Prospect Theory, Rational Choice, and International Relations."

68. Hakes, *Declaration of Energy Independence*, 70.

69. Hardin, "Extensions of the 'Tragedy of the Commons.'"

70. Ostrom, "Coping with Tragedies of the Commons."

71. Ibid.; see also Milinski et al., "Reputation Helps Solve the 'Tragedy of the Commons,'" 424–26.

### Conclusion · *Making Better Decisions*

1. West, Meserve, and Stanovich, "Cognitive Sophistication Does Not Attenuate the Bias Blind Spot."

2. Arnott, "Cognitive Biases and Decision Support Systems Development."

3. Schafer and Crichlow, *Groupthink versus High-Quality Decision Making in International Relations*.

4. Kahneman and Renshon, "Why Hawks Win."

5. Hilbert, "Toward a Synthesis of Cognitive Biases."

6. Larrick, "Debiasing," 317.

7. Stanovich and West, "Individual Differences in Reasoning." See also Epstein, "Integration of the Cognitive and Psychodynamic Unconscious."

8. Allison and Zelikow, *Essence of Decision*, 13, 15–17.

9. See Tetlock, *Expert Political Judgment.*

10. For an example of rationality in business, see Forman and Selly, *Decision by Objectives,* chap. 8.

11. Ibid., 143.

12. See Baron, *Thinking and Deciding.*

13. Krause, "High Reliability Performance Cognitive Biases Undermine Decision Making."

14. Kennedy, *Thirteen Days,* 86.

15. George and Stern, "Harnessing Conflict in Foreign Policy Making," 488.

16. Ibid.

17. Bazerman, White, and Loewenstein, "Perceptions of Fairness in Interpersonal and Individual Choice Situations."

18. Bazerman, Loewenstein, and White, "Reversals of Preference in Allocation Decisions."

19. Moore and Loewenstein, "Self-Interest, Automaticity, and the Psychology of Conflict of Interest."

20. Stein, "Foreign Policy Decision-Making."

21. Larrick, "Debiasing."

22. Renshon, *Psychological Assessment of Presidential Candidates.*

23. See Zak, *Moral Molecule.*

24. Milkman, Rogers, and Bazerman, "Harnessing Our Inner Angels and Demons."

25. Ibid. On problems with this approach, see Dunlosky and Metcalfe, *Metacognition,* 123–25.

26. On this literature, see Clemen and Lichtendahl, "Debiasing Expert Overconfidence."

27. Larrick, "Debiasing," 324.

28. Renshon and Renshon, "Enduring Legacy of Alexander L. George."

29. Koehler, Gibbs, and Hogarth, "Shattering the Illusion of Control," 183.

30. Gigerenzer and Hoffrage, "How to Improve Bayesian Reasoning without Instruction."

31. Larrick, "Debiasing," 325.

32. Ibid., 324–25.

33. Tetlock, *Expert Political Judgment,* 40, 77.

34. See Tversky and Kahneman, "Extensional versus Intuitive Reasoning."

35. For such analysis, see Page and Clemen, "Do Prediction Markets Produce Well-Calibrated Probability Forecasts?"

36. See Reese, "Techniques for Mitigating Cognitive Biases in Fingerprint Identification," 1252; Dunlosky and Metcalfe, *Metacognition,* 126–28.

37. Kahneman and Tversky, "Intuitive Prediction."

38. Ibid.

39. Ibid.

40. Flyvbjerg, *Procedures for Dealing with Optimism Bias in Transport Planning.*

41. Flyvbjerg, "Curbing Optimism Bias and Strategic Misrepresentation in Planning."

42. Kahneman, *Thinking, Fast and Slow,* 251.

43. Tetlock, *Expert Political Judgment,* 129, 137.

44. Jamieson and Cappella, *Echo Chamber.*

45. Maccoun, "Biases in the Interpretation and Use of Research Results."

46. This paragraph is based on Swann, Pelham, and Krull, "Agreeable Fancy or Dis-

agreeable Truth?" and White, Brockett, and Overstreet, "Confirmatory Bias in Evaluating Personality Test Information."

47. See, for instance, Parmley, "Effects of the Confirmation Bias on Diagnostic Decision Making."

48. Tversky and Kahneman, "Advances in Prospect Theory."

49. "Cartoon Stickers May Sway Kids' Food Choices: Study," Reuters, August 22, 2012, http://reuters.com/article/2012/08/22/us-stickers-idUSBRE87L0LI20120822.

50. Thaler and Sunstein, *Nudge*.

51. Benartzi and Thaler, "Heuristics and Biases in Retirement Savings Behavior."

52. See Kahneman, *Thinking, Fast and Slow*.

53. Ibid.

54. Tversky and Kahneman, "Framing of Decisions and the Psychology of Choice."

55. Schwartz, *Paradox of Choice*.

56. van de Ven, Gilovich, and Zeelenberg, "Delay, Doubt, and Decision."

57. See Sevdalis and Harvey, "Reducing the Impact Bias in Judgments of Post-Decisional Affect."

58. See Yetiv, *Explaining Foreign Policy*.

59. Larrick, "Debiasing."

60. Janis, *Groupthink*, 9.

61. Ibid., 247.

62. Yetiv, *Explaining Foreign Policy*.

63. Larrick, "Debiasing," 327.

64. Mesmer-Magnus and DeChurch, "Information Sharing and Team Performance."

65. Ibid., 535–46.

66. Cited in Kahler, "Rationality in International Relations," 927.

67. See Khong, *Analogies at War*, 10. For conditions under which cognitive factors such as historical analogies are likely to be influential in decision making, see George, *Presidential Decisionmaking in Foreign Policy*, chaps. 2–3. Also, Neustadt and May, *Thinking in Time*.

68. Bazerman and Chugh, "Bounded Awareness."

69. On this literature, see Wallace, Suedfeld, and Thachuk, "Political Rhetoric of Leaders under Stress in the Gulf Crisis." On the impact of stress, see also Janis and Mann, *Decision Making*.

70. On how analogies are used and misused, see Vertzberger, *World in Their Minds*, esp. chap. 6; and Jervis, *Perception and Misperception in International Policy*, 220, 237.

71. Lilienfeld, Ammirati, and Landfield, "Giving Debiasing Away."

72. Tetlock, "Accountability and the Perseverance of First Impressions," 232.

73. Alker, *Rediscoveries and Reformulations*.

74. Savitsky and Gilovich, "Illusion of Transparency and the Alleviation of Speech Anxiety."

75. Edwards and Fasolo, *Decision Technology*, 581.

76. Silverman, "Modeling and Critiquing the Confirmation Bias in Human Reasoning."

77. Cook and Smallman, "Human Factors of the Confirmation Bias in Intelligence Analysis."

78. Stanovich and West, "Individual Differences in Reasoning."

79. On these obstacles, see Lilienfeld, Ammirati, and Landfield, "Giving Debiasing Away," 394–96.

Alker, Hayward. *Rediscoveries and Reformulations: Humanistic Methodologies for International Studies.* New York: Cambridge University Press, 1996.

Allison, Graham T., and Philip Zelikow. *Essence of Decision: Explaining the Cuban Missile Crisis.* New York: Longman, 1999.

Arana, Jorge E., and Carmelo J. Leon. "Understanding the Use of Non-Compensatory Decision Rules in Discrete Choice Experiments: The Role of Emotions." *Ecological Economics* 68 (2009): 2316–26.

Ariely, Dan. *Predictably Irrational: The Hidden Forces That Shape Our Decisions.* New York: Harper, 2008.

———. *The Upside of Irrationality: The Unexpected Benefits of Defying Logic at Work and at Home.* New York: Harper, 2010.

Arnott, David. "Cognitive Biases and Decision Support Systems Development: A Design Science Approach." *Information Systems Journal* 16 (2006): 55–78.

Bacevich, Andrew J., and Elizabeth H. Prodromou. "God Is Not Neutral: Religion and U.S. Foreign Policy after 9/11." *Orbis* 48 (2004): 43–54.

Barber, Brad M., and Terrance Odean. "Boys Will Be Boys: Gender, Overconfidence, and Common Stock Investment." *Quarterly Journal of Economics* 116 (2001): 261–92.

Baron, Jonathan. *Thinking and Deciding.* Cambridge: Cambridge University Press, 2008.

Bazerman, Max H., and Dolly Chugh. "Bounded Awareness: Focusing Failures in Negotiation." In *Negotiation Theory and Research*, edited by Leigh Thompson, 7–26. New York: Psychology Press, 2005.

Bazerman, Max H., George F. Loewenstein, and Sally Blount White. "Reversals of Preference in Allocation Decisions: Judging an Alternative versus Choosing among Alternatives." *Administrative Science Quarterly* 37 (1992): 220–40.

Bazerman, Max H., Sally Blount White, and George F. Loewenstein. "Perceptions of Fairness in Interpersonal and Individual Choice Situations." *Current Directions in Psychological Science* 4 (1995): 39–43.

Belasco, Amy. "The Cost of Iraq, Afghanistan, and Other Global War on Terror Operations Since 9/11." Washington, DC: Congressional Research Service, 2011.

Benartzi, Shlomo, and Richard H. Thaler. "Heuristics and Biases in Retirement Savings Behavior." *Journal of Economic Perspectives* 21 (2007): 81–104.

Benjamin, Daniel, and Steven Simon. *The Age of Sacred Terror.* New York: Random House, 2002.

Bensahel, Nora. "Mission Not Accomplished." In *War in Iraq: Planning and Execution*, edited by Thomas G. Mahnken and Thomas A. Keaney, 250–80. London: Routledge, 2007.

Beresteanu, Arie, and Shanjun Li. "Gasoline Prices, Government Support, and the Demand for Hybrid Vehicles in the United States." *International Economic Review* 52 (2011): 161–82.

Bergen, Peter L. *Holy War, Inc.: Inside the Secret World of Osama bin Laden*. New York: Free Press, 2001.

Bodansky, Yossef. *Bin Laden: The Man Who Declared War on America*. Rocklin, CA: Forum, 1999.

Borjesson, Kristina, ed. *Feet to the Fire: The Media after 9/11. Top Journalists Speak Out*. New York: Prometheus Books, 2005.

Bostrom, Nick, and Toby Ord. "The Reversal Test: Eliminating Status Quo Bias in Applied Ethics." *Ethics* 116 (2006): 656–79.

Bradsher, Henry S. "The Soviet Union and the War in Afghanistan." In *The Soviet Union and the Third World*, edited by Carol R. Saivetz, 128–49. Boulder, CO: Westview, 1989.

———. *Afghanistan and the Soviet Union*. Durham, NC: Duke University Press, 1983.

Brands, Hal. "*Inside* the Iraqi State Records: Saddam Hussein, 'Irangate,' and the United States." Journal of Strategic Studies 34 (2011): 95–118.

Brecher, Michael. "State Behavior in a Crisis: A Model." *Journal of Conflict Resolution* 23 (1979): 446–80.

Brisard, Jean-Charles, and Damien Martinez. *Zarqawi: The New Face of al-Qaeda*. New York: Other Press, 2005.

Buehler, Roger, Dale Griffin, and Michael Ross. "Exploring the 'Planning Fallacy': Why People Underestimate Their Task Completion Times." *Journal of Personality and Social Psychology* 67 (1994): 366–81.

Bukszar, Ed. "Does Overconfidence Lead to Poor Decisions?: A Comparison of Decision Making and Judgment under Uncertainty." *Journal of Business and Management* (2003): 33–43.

Bush, George W. *Decision Points*. New York: Crown, 2010.

Camerer, Colin, George Loewenstein, and Drazen Prelec. "Neuroeconomics: How Neuroscience Can Inform Economics." *Journal of Economic Literature* 43 (2005): 9–64.

Carter, Jimmy. *Keeping Faith: Memoirs of a President*. New York: Bantam Books, 1982.

———. *Public Papers of the Presidents of the United States, Jimmy Carter*. Washington, DC: U.S. Government Printing Office.

Castano, Emanuele, Simona Sacchi, and Peter Hays Gries. "The Perception of the Other in International Relations: Evidence for the Polarizing Effect of Entitativity." *Political Psychology* 24 (2003): 449–68.

Chabris, Christopher F., and Daniel J. Simons. *The Invisible Gorilla: And Other Ways Our Intuitions Deceive Us*. New York: Crown, 2010.

Clancy, Tom, Anthony C. Zinni, and Tony Koltz. *Battle Ready*. New York: Putnam, 2004.

Clarke, Richard A. *Against All Enemies: Inside America's War on Terror*. New York: Free Press, 2004.

Clemen, Robert T., and Kenneth C. Lichtendahl Jr. "Debiasing Expert Overconfidence: A Bayesian Calibration Model." Paper presented at the International Conference on Probabilistic Safety Assessment and Management, San Juan, Puerto Rico, June 27, 2002.

Coll, Steve. *Ghost Wars: The Secret History of the CIA, Afghanistan, and bin Laden, from the Soviet Invasion to September 10, 2001.* New York: Penguin, 2004.

Cook, Maia B., and Harvey S. Smallman. "Human Factors of the Confirmation Bias in Intelligence Analysis: Decision Support from Graphical Evidence Landscapes." *Human Factors* 50 (2008): 745–54.

Cordesman, Anthony H. *The Iran–Iraq War and Western Security, 1984–87: Strategic Implications and Policy Options.* London: Jane's Information Group, 1987.

Cordovez, Diego, and Selig S. Harrison. *Out of Afghanistan: The Insider Story of the Soviet Withdrawal.* New York: Oxford University Press, 1995.

De Angelis, Paul, and Elisabeth Kaestner, trans. *Inside 9-11: What Really Happened.* New York: St. Martin's, 2002.

de Mesquita, Bruce Bueno, and Rose McDermott. "Crossing No Man's Land: Cooperation from the Trenches." *Political Psychology* 25 (2004): 271–87.

DeYoung, Karen. *Soldier: The Life of Colin Powell.* New York: Alfred A. Knopf, 2006.

Diamond, David. "The Impact of Government Incentives for Hybrid-Electric Vehicles: Evidence from US States." *Energy Policy* 37 (2009): 972–83.

Diamond, John, Judy Keen, David Moniz, Susan Page, and Barbara Slavin. "Iraq Course Set from Tight White House Circle." *USA Today,* September 11, 2002.

Dobrynin, Anatoly. *In Confidence: Moscow's Ambassador to America's Six Cold War Presidents, 1962–1986.* New York: Times Books, 1995.

Draper, Robert. *Dead Certain: The Presidency of George W. Bush.* New York: Free Press, 2007.

Duelfer, Charles A., and Stephen Benedict Dyson, "Chronic Misperception and International Conflict: The U.S.–Iraq Experience." *International Security* 36 (2011): 73–100.

Duffield, John S. *Over a Barrel: The Costs of U.S. Foreign Oil Dependence.* Stanford, CA: Stanford University Press, 2008.

Dunlosky, John, and Janet Metcalfe. *Metacognition: A Textbook for Cognitive, Educational, Lifespan and Applied Psychology.* Thousand Oaks, CA: Sage, 2009.

Edwards, Ward, and Barbara Fasolo. "Decision Technology." *Annual Review of Psychology* 52 (2001): 581–606.

Epstein, Seymour. "Integration of the Cognitive and the Psychodynamic Unconscious." *American Psychologist* 49 (1994): 709–24.

Fandy, Mamoun. *Saudi Arabia and the Politics of Dissent.* New York: St. Martin's, 1999.

Farnham, Barbara. "Roosevelt and the Munich Crisis: Insights from Prospect Theory." *Political Psychology* 13 (1992): 205–35.

Feith, Douglas J. *War and Decision: Inside the Pentagon at the Dawn of the War on Terrorism.* New York: Harper, 2008.

Fernandez, Raquel, and Dani Rodrik. "Resistance to Reform: Status Quo Bias in the Presence of Individual-Specific Uncertainty." *American Economic Review* 81 (1991): 1146–55.

Fischhoff, Baruch. "Debiasing." In *Judgment under Uncertainty: Heuristics and Biases,* edited by Daniel Kahneman, Peter Slovic, and Amos Tversky, 422–44. Cambridge: Cambridge University Press, 1982.

Flyvbjerg, Bent. "Curbing Optimism Bias and Strategic Misrepresentation in Planning: Reference Class Forecasting in Practice." *European Planning Studies* 16 (2008): 3–21.

Flyvbjerg, Bent, and COWI. *Procedures for Dealing with Optimism Bias in Transport Planning: Guidance Document.* London: UK Department for Transport, 2004.

Forman, Ernest H., and Mary Ann Selly. *Decision by Objectives: How to Convince Others That You Are Right*. River Edge, NJ: World Scientific, 2001.

Frey, Bruno S. *Inspiring Economics: Human Motivation in Political Economy*. Cheltenham, UK: Edward Elgar, 2001.

Frey, Bruno S., and Alois Stutzer, *Happiness and Economics*. Princeton, NJ: Princeton University Press, 2002.

Freyberg-Inan, Annette, Ewan Harrison, and Patrick James, eds. *Rethinking Realism in International Relations: Between Tradition and Innovation*. Baltimore: Johns Hopkins University Press, 2009.

Fuller, Graham E. *The Future of Political Islam*. New York: Palgrave, 2003.

George, Alexander L. *Presidential Decisionmaking in Foreign Policy: The Effective Use of Information and Advice*. Boulder, CO: Westview Press, 1980.

George, Alexander L., and Eric K. Stern. "Harnessing Conflict in Foreign Policy Making: From Devil's to Multiple Advocacy." *Presidential Studies Quarterly* 32 (2002): 484–505.

Gigerenzer, Gerd. *Adaptive Thinking: Rationality in the Real World*. Oxford: Oxford University Press, 2000.

Gigerenzer, Gerd, and Ulrich Hoffrage. "How to Improve Bayesian Reasoning without Instruction: Frequency Formats." *Psychological Review* 102 (1995): 684–705.

Gilovich, Thomas. *How We Know What Isn't So: The Fallibility of Human Reason in Everyday Life*. New York: Free Press, 1991.

Goertz, Gary. "Constraints, Compromises, and Decision Making." *Journal of Conflict Resolution* 48 (2004): 14–37.

Goldgeier, J. M., and Philip E. Tetlock. "Psychology and International Relations Theory." *Annual Review of Political Science* 4 (2001): 67–92.

Gordon, Michael R., and Bernard E. Trainor. *The Endgame: The Inside Story of the Struggle for Iraq, from George W. Bush to Barack Obama*. New York: Pantheon, 2012.

Gray, Jeremy R. "A Bias toward Short-Term Thinking in Threat-Related Negative Emotional States." *Personality and Social Psychology Bulletin* 25 (1999): 65–75.

Green, Donald P., and Ian Shapiro, *Pathologies of Rational Choice Theory: A Critique of Applications on Political Science*. New Haven, CT: Yale University Press, 1994.

Griffin, Dale W., David Dunning, and Lee Ross. "The Role of Construal Processes in Overconfident Predictions about the Self and Others." *Journal of Personality and Social Psychology* 59 (1990): 1128–39.

Gromyko, Andrei. *Memoirs*. New York: Doubleday, 1989.

Haas, Mark. "Prospect Theory and the Cuban Missile Crisis." *International Studies Quarterly* 45 (2001): 241–70.

Haass, Richard. *War of Necessity: War of Choice*. New York: Simon & Schuster, 2009.

Hafez, Mohammed M. *Why Muslims Rebel: Repression and Resistance in the Islamic World*. Boulder, CO: Lynne Rienner, 2003.

Hakes, Jay E. *A Declaration of Energy Independence: How Freedom from Foreign Oil Can Improve National Security, Our Economy, and the Environment*. Hoboken, NJ: Wiley, 2008.

Halliday, Fred. *Soviet Policy in the Arc of Crisis*. Amsterdam: Netherlands Institute for Policy Studies, 1981.

Hammond, Thomas T. *Red Flag over Afghanistan*. Boulder, CO: Westview Press, 1984.

Hardin, Garrett. "Extensions of the 'Tragedy of the Commons.'" *Science* (1988) 280: 682–83.

———. "The Tragedy of the Commons." *Science* 162 (1968): 1243–48.

Hastie, Reid, and Robyn M. Dawes. *Rational Choice in an Uncertain World: The Psychology of Judgment and Decision Making.* Thousand Oaks, CA: Sage, 2001.

Hawkins, S. A., and Reid Hastie. "Hindsight: Biased Judgments of Past Events after the Outcomes Are Known." *Psychological Bulletin* 107 (1990): 311–27.

Heffner, Reid R., Kenneth S. Kurani, and Thomas S. Turrentine. "Symbolism in California's Early Market for Hybrid Electric Vehicles." Davis, CA: Institute of Transportation Studies, University of California, 2008.

Heinen, Joel T., and Roberta S. Low. "Human Behavioral Ecology and Environmental Conservation." *Environmental Conservation* 19 (1992): 105–16.

Herrmann, Richard K., and Michael P. Fischerkeller. "Beyond the Enemy Image and Spiral Model: Cognitive-Strategic Research after the Cold War." *International Organization* 49 (1995): 415–50.

Hershberg, James G., ed. "Meeting of the CC CPUS Politburo, 27 April 1978." *Cold War International History Project Bulletin* 8/9 (1996): 112–13.

Hilbert, Martin. "Toward a Synthesis of Cognitive Biases: How Noisy Information Processing Can Bias Human Decision Making." *Psychological Bulletin* 138 (2012): 211–37.

Holland, Emily. "The Soviet Invasion of Afghanistan: Superpower Crisis and the 'Second Cold War.'" *Columbia Undergraduate Journal of History*, 2008, 1–12.

Holt, Mark, and Carol Glover. "Energy Policy Act of 2005: Summary and Analysis of Enacted Provisions." Washington, DC: Congressional Research Service, 2006.

Hood, Bruce. *SuperSense: Why We Believe in the Unbelievable.* New York: HarperOne, 2009.

Horowitz, Daniel. *Jimmy Carter and the Energy Crisis of the 1970s.* New York: St. Martin's, 2005.

Hudson, Valerie. "Foreign Policy Analysis: Actor-Specific Theory and the Ground of International Relations." *Foreign Policy Analysis* 1 (2005): 1–30.

Hurwitz, Jon, Mark Peffley, and Mitchell A. Seligson. "Foreign Policy Belief Systems in Comparative Perspective: The United States and Costa Rica." *International Studies Quarterly* 37 (1993): 245–70.

Hussein, Saddam, and Ofra Bengio. *Saddam Speaks on the Gulf Crisis: A Collection of Documents.* Tel Aviv: Shiloah Institute, 1992.

Ibrahim, Raymond, Ayman Zawahiri, and Osama bin Laden. *The al-Qaeda Reader.* New York: Doubleday, 2007.

Ibroscheva, Elza. "Is There Still an Evil Empire? The Role of the Mass Media in Depicting Stereotypes of Russians and Eastern Europeans." *Global Media Journal* 1 (2002): Article 11.

Jamieson, Kathleen Hall, and Joseph N. Cappella. *Echo Chamber: Rush Limbaugh and the Conservative Media Establishment.* New York: Oxford University Press, 2008.

Janis, Irving L. *Groupthink: Psychological Studies of Policy Decisions and Fiascoes.* Boston: Wadsworth, 1982.

Janis, Irving L., and Leon Mann. *Decision Making: A Psychological Analysis of Conflict, Choice, and Commitment.* New York: Free Press, 1977.

Jenkins, Brian Michael. *Will Terrorists Go Nuclear?* New York: Prometheus Books, 2008.

Jervis, Robert. *Perception and Misperception in International Politics.* Princeton, NJ: Princeton University Press, 1976.

———. "Cooperation under the Security Dilemma." *World Politics* 30 (1978): 167–214.

———. "Deterrence and Perception." *International Security* 7 (1982/83): 3–30.

———. "Perceiving and Coping with Threat." In *Psychology and Deterrence*, edited by Robert Jervis, Richard Ned Lebow, and Janice Gross Stein, 13–33. Baltimore: Johns Hopkins University Press, 1985.

Johnson, Dominic D. P., *Overconfidence and War: The Havoc and Glory of Positive Illusions*. Cambridge, MA: Harvard University Press, 2004.

Johnson, Dominic D. P., Rose McDermott, Emily S. Barrett, Jonathan Cowden, Richard Wrangham, Matthew H. McIntyre, and Stephen Peter Rosen. "Overconfidence in War Games: Experimental Evidence on Expectations, Aggression, Gender and Testosterone." *Proceedings of the Royal Society B: Biological Sciences* 273 (2006): 2513–20.

Johnson, Thomas H. "Financing Afghan Terrorism: Thugs, Drugs, and Creative Movements of Money." In *Terrorism Financing and State Responses: A Comparative Perspective*, edited by Jeanne K. Giraldo and Harold A. Trinkunas, 93–114. Stanford, CA: Stanford University Press.

Jones, Martin, and Robert Sugden. "Positive Confirmation Bias in the Acquisition of Information." *Theory and Decision* 50 (2001): 59–99.

Juergensmeyer, Mark. *Terror in the Mind of God: The Global Rise of the Religious Violence.* Berkeley, CA: University of California Press, 2000.

———. "Religious Terror and Global War." In *Understanding September 11*, edited by Craig Calhoun, 27–40. New York: New Press, 2002.

Juhasz, Antonia. *The Tyranny of Oil: The World's Most Powerful Industry—And What We Must Do to Stop It.* New York: William Morrow, 2008.

Kahler, Miles. "Rationality in International Relations." *International Organization* 52 (1998): 919–41.

Kahn, Matthew E. "Do Greens Drive Hummers or Hybrids? Environmental Ideology as a Determinant of Consumer Choice." *Journal of Environmental Economics and Management* 54 (2007): 129–45.

Kahneman, Daniel. *Thinking, Fast and Slow.* New York: Farrar, Straus and Giroux, 2011.

Kahneman, Daniel, and Jonathan Renshon. "Why Hawks Win." *Foreign Policy*, December 27, 2006.

Kahneman, Daniel, and Amos Tversky. "Intuitive Prediction: Biases and Corrective Procedures." In *Forecasting: Studies in Management Sciences*, edited by Spyros G. Makridakis and Steven C. Wheelwright, 313–27. Amsterdam: North Holland, 1979.

———. *Choices, Values, and Frames.* New York: Russell Sage Foundation, 2000.

Kahneman, Daniel, Jack L. Knetsch, and Richard H. Thaler. "Anomalies: The Endowment Effect, Loss Aversion, and Status Quo Bias." *Journal of Economic Perspectives* 5 (1991): 193–206.

Kahneman, Daniel, Alan B. Krueger, David Schkade, Norbert Schwartz, and Arthur A. Stone. "Would You Be Happier If You Were Richer? A Focusing Illusion." *Science* 312 (2006): 1908–10.

Kahneman, Daniel, Paul Slovic, and Amos Tversky. *Judgment under Uncertainty: Heuristics and Biases.* Cambridge: Cambridge University Press, 1982.

Karam, Azza M. *Transnational Political Islam: Religion, Ideology, and Power.* London: Pluto Press, 2004.

Kaufman, Burton Ira. *The Presidency of James Earl Carter, Jr.* Lawrence: University Press of Kansas, 1993.

Kaufmann, Chaim. "Threat Inflation and the Failure of the Marketplace of Ideas: The Selling of the Iraq War." *International Security* 29 (2004): 5–48.

Kennedy, Robert F. *Thirteen Days: A Memoir of the Cuban Missile Crisis.* New York: Norton, 1969.

Kepel, Gilles. *Jihad: The Trail of Political Islam.* Cambridge, MA: Harvard University Press, 2002.

Kepel, Gilles, and Jean-Pierre Milelli, eds. *Al-Qaeda in Its Own Words.* Cambridge, MA: Belknap, 2008.

Khalil, Elias L. *The New Behavioral Economics.* Cheltenham, UK: Edward Elgar, 2009.

Khan, M. A. Muqtedar. "Radical Islam, Liberal Islam." *Current History* 102 (2003): 417–21.

Khong, Yuen Foong. *Analogies at War: Korea, Munich, Dien Bien Phu, and the Vietnam Decisions of 1965.* Princeton, NJ: Princeton University Press, 1992.

Kida, Thomas. *Don't Believe Everything You Think: The 6 Basic Mistakes We Make in Thinking.* New York: Prometheus Books, 2006.

Klare, Michael T. *Blood and Oil: The Dangers and Consequences of America's Growing Petroleum Dependency.* New York: Metropolitan Books, 2004.

Koehler, Jonathan J., Brian J. Gibbs, and Robin M. Hogarth. "Shattering the Illusion of Control: Multi-Shot versus Single-Shot Games." *Journal of Behavioral Decision Making* 7 (1994): 183–91.

Krause, Thomas R. "High Reliability Performance Cognitive Biases Undermine Decision Making." *Industrial Safety & Hygiene News,* September 1, 2010.

Kruger, Justin, and David Dunning, "Unskilled and Unaware of It: How Difficulties in Recognizing One's Own Incompetence Lead to Inflated Self-Assessments." *Journal of Personality and Social Psychology* 77 (1999): 1121–34.

Langer, Ellen J. "The Psychology of Chance." *Journal for the Theory of Social Behavior* 7 (1977): 185–203.

Laqueur, Walter, ed. *Voices of Terror: Manifestos, Writings, and Manuals of al Qaeda, Hamas, and Other Terrorists from around the World and throughout the Ages.* New York: Reed Press, 2004.

Larrick, Richard P. "Debiasing." In *Blackwell Handbook of Judgment and Decision Making,* edited by Derek J. Koehler and Nigel Harvey, 316–38. Malden, MA: Blackwell, 2004.

Lebow, Richard Ned. "Deterrence: A Political and Psychological Critique." In *Perspectives on Deterrence,* edited by Paul C. Stern, Robert Axelrod, Robert Jervis, and Roy Radner, 25–51. Oxford: Oxford University Press, 1989.

Lesch, David W. *1979: The Year That Shaped the Modern Middle East.* Boulder, CO: Westview Press, 2001.

Levy, Jack. "Prospect Theory, Rational Choice, and International Relations." *International Studies Quarterly* 41 (1997): 87–112.

Levy, Jack. "Political Psychology and Foreign Policy." In *Oxford Handbook of Political Psychology,* edited by David O. Sears, Leonie Huddy, and Robert Jervis, 254–84. Oxford: Oxford University Press, 2003.

Lilienfeld, Scott O., Rachel Ammirati, and Kristin Landfield. "Giving Debiasing Away: Can Psychological Research on Correcting Cognitive Errors Promote Human Welfare?" *Perspectives on Psychological Science* 4 (2009): 390–98.

Lowe, Robert, and Arvids A. Ziedonis. "Overoptimism and the Performance of Entrepreneurial Firms." *Management Science* 52 (2006): 173–86.

Lynch, Marc. "Anti-Americanisms in the Arab World." *Anti-Americanisms in World Politics.* Ithaca, NY: Cornell University Press, 2007.

Maccoun, Robert J. "Biases in the Interpretation and Use of Research Results." *Annual Review of Psychology* 49 (1998): 259–87.

Malkiel, Burton G. *A Random Walk down Wall Street.* New York: W.W. Norton, 2003.

Mankiw, N. Gregory. "Gas Tax Now!" *Fortune,* May 24, 1999.

———. "Greenspan on Gas Taxes." *Greg Mankiw's Blog: Random Observations for Students of Economics* (blog), October 2, 2006, http://gregmankiw.blogspot.com/2006/10/green span-on-gas-taxes.html.

———. "Raise the Gas Tax." *Wall Street Journal,* October 20, 2006.

Mann, Jim. *Rise of the Vulcans: The History of Bush's War Cabinet.* New York: Viking, 2004.

Manuck, Stephen B., et al. "A Neurobiology of Intertemporal Choice." In *Time and Decision: Economic Psychological Perspectives on Intertemporal Choice,* edited by George Loewenstein, Daniel Read, and Roy F. Baumeister, 139–73. New York: Sage, 2003.

Massari, Paul. "Of Two Minds." *Harvard Gazette,* December 7, 2010, http://news.harvard .edu/gazette/story/2010/12/of-two-minds/.

McDermott, Rose. "Experimental Methods in Political Science." *Annual Review of Political Science* 5 (2002): 325–42.

———. "The Feeling of Rationality: The Meaning of Neuroscientific Advances for Political Science." *Perspectives on Politics* 2 (2004): 691–706.

———. *Political Psychology in International Relations.* Ann Arbor: University of Michigan Press, 2004.

McDermott, Rose, Nicole Wernimont, and Cheryl Koopman. "Applying Psychology to International Studies: Prospects and Challenges in Interdisciplinary Work." *International Studies Perspectives* 12 (2011): 119–35.

McGraw, Peter, Barbara A. Mellers, and Ilana Ritov. "The Affective Costs of Overconfidence." *Journal of Behavioral Decision Making* 17 (2004): 281–95.

McKenzie, Craig R. M. "Judgment and Decision Making." In *Handbook of Cognition,* edited by Koen Lamberts and Robert L. Goldstone, 321–38. London: Sage, 2005.

Mercer, Jonathan. "Rationality and Psychology in International Politics." *International Organization* 59 (2005): 77–106.

Mesmer-Magnus, Jessica, and Leslie DeChurch. "Information Sharing and Team Performance: A Meta-Analysis." *Journal of Applied Psychology* 94 (2009): 535–46.

Milinski, Manfred, Dirk Semmann, and Hans-Jurgen Krambeck. "Reputation Helps Solve the 'Tragedy of the Commons.'" *Nature* 415 (2002): 424–26.

Milkman, Katherine L., Dolly Chugh, and Max H. Bazerman, "How Can Decision Making Be Improved?" *Perspectives on Psychological Science* 4 (2009): 379–83.

Milkman, Katherine L., Todd Rogers, and Max H. Bazerman, "Harnessing Our Inner Angels and Demons: What We Have Learned about Want/Should Conflicts and How That Knowledge Can Help Us Reduce Short-Sighted Decision Making." *Perspectives on Psychological Science* 3 (2008): 324–38.

Miller, Sunlen. "Obama: We Can't 'Hit the Snooze Button' When Gas Prices Fall Again." *ABC News,* March 30, 2011.

Mintz, Alex. "The Decision to Attack Iraq: A Noncompensatory Theory of Decision Making." *Journal of Conflict Resolution* (1993): 595–618.

———. "Foreign Policy Decision Making: Bridging the Gap Between the Cognitive Psychology and Rational Actor 'Schools.'" In *Decisionmaking on War and Peace: The Cognitive-Rational Debate*, edited by Nehemia Geva and Alex Mintz, 1–10. Boulder, CO: Lynne Rienner, 1997.

———. "How Do Leaders Make Decisions? A Poliheuristic Perspective." *Journal of Conflict Resolution* 48 (2004): 3–13.

Mintz, Alex, and Karl DeRouen Jr. *Understanding Foreign Policy Decision Making*. New York: Cambridge University Press, 2010.

Mintz, Alex, and Nehemia Geva. "The Poliheuristic Theory of Foreign Policy Decisionmaking." In *Decision Making on War and Peace: The Cognitive-Rational Debate*, edited by Nehemia Geva and Alex Mintz, 81–101. Boulder, CO: Lynne Rienner, 1997.

Mitchell, David, and Tansa George Massoud. "Anatomy of Failure: Bush's Decision-Making Process and the Iraq War." *Foreign Policy Analysis* 5 (2009): 265–86.

Moghadam, Assaf. "Motives for Martyrdom: Al-Qaida, Salafi Jihad, and the Spread of Suicide Attacks." *International Security* 33 (2008): 46–78.

Montier, James. *Behavioural Finance: Insights into Irrational Minds and Markets*. Hoboken, NJ: Wiley, 2002.

———. *Behavioural Investing: A Practitioner's Guide to Applying Behavioural Financing*. Hoboken, NJ: Wiley, 2007.

Moore, Don A., and Paul J. Healy. "The Trouble with Overconfidence." *Psychological Review* 115 (2008): 502–17.

Moore, Don A., and George F. Loewenstein. "Self Interest, Automaticity, and the Psychology of Conflict of Interest." *Social Justice Research* 17 (2004): 189–202.

Moran, Daniel, and James Russell. *Energy Security and Global Politics: The Militarization of Resource Management*. New York: Routledge, 2008.

Murawiec, Laurent. *The Mind of Jihad*. Cambridge: Cambridge University Press, 2008.

Myers, Richard B. *Eyes on the Horizon: Serving on the Frontlines of National Security*. New York: Threshold, 2009.

Neustadt, Richard E., and Ernest R. May. *Thinking in Time: The Uses of History for Decision Makers*. New York: Free Press, 1986.

Nimitz, Matthew. "U.S. Security Framework." *Current Policy* 221 (1980): 1–4.

Nisbett, Richard, and Lee Ross. *Human Inference: Strategies and Shortcomings of Social Judgment*. Englewood Cliffs, NJ: Prentice-Hall, 1980.

Odean, Terrance. "Volume, Volatility, Price, and Profit: When All Traders Are above Average." *Journal of Finance* (1998): 1887–934.

Ostrom, Elinor. *Governing the Commons: The Evolution of Institutions for Collective Action*. Cambridge: Cambridge University Press, 1990.

———. "Coping with Tragedies of the Commons." *Annual Review of Political Science* 2 (1999): 493–535.

Ostrom, Elinor, Roy Gardner, and James Walker. *Rules, Games, and Common–Pool Resources*. Ann Arbor: University of Michigan Press, 1994.

Page, Lionel, and Robert T. Clemen. "Do Prediction Markets Produce Well-Calibrated Probability Forecasts?" *Economic Journal* 122 (2012): doi:10.1111/j.1468-0297.2012.02561.x.

Pape, Robert Anthony. *Dying to Win: The Strategic Logic of Suicide Terrorism*. New York: Random House, 2005.

Parmley, Meagan Carleton. "The Effects of the Confirmation Bias on Diagnostic Decision Making." PhD thesis, Drexel University, 2006.

Perl, Raphael. "Terrorism, the Future, and U.S. Foreign Policy." Washington, DC: Congressional Research Service, 1996.

Peters, Edward. "The Firanj Are Coming—Again." *Orbis* 48 (2004): 3–17.

Pfiffner, James P. "Did President Bush Mislead the Country in His Arguments for War with Iraq?" *Presidential Studies Quarterly* 34 (2004): 25–46.

Pillar, Paul R. "Intelligence, Policy, and the War in Iraq." *Foreign Affairs*, March/April 2006.

———. *Intelligence and U.S. Foreign Policy: Iraq, 9/11, and Misguided Reform*. New York: Columbia University Press, 2011.

Pollack, Kenneth M. *The Persian Puzzle: The Conflict between Iran and America*. New York: Random House, 2004.

Powell, Colin L., and Joseph E. Persico. *My American Journey*. New York: Random House, 1995.

Qutb, Sayyid. *Milestones*. Damascus: Dar al-Ilm, 2000.

Ramachandran, V. S., and Sandra Blakelee. *Phantoms in the Brain: Probing the Mysteries of the Human Mind*. New York: William Morrow, 1998.

Rashid, Ahmed. *Taliban: Militant Islam, Oil, and Fundamentalism in Central Asia*. New Haven, CT: Yale University Press, 2000.

Reagan, Ronald. "Address to the Nation on the Iran Arms and Contra Aid Controversy, March 4, 1987." Simi Valley, CAL Ronald Reagan Presidential Foundation and Library, http://www.reagan.utexas.edu/archives/speeches/1987/030487h.htm, 1987.

———. *Public Papers of the Presidents of the United States, Ronald Reagan*. Washington, DC: U.S. Government Printing Office.

———. "Remarks at the Annual Convention of the National Association of Evangelicals in Orlando Florida, March 8, 1983." Santa Barbara: The American Presidency Project, University of California, 1983.

Reese, Elizabeth J. "Techniques for Mitigating Cognitive Biases in Fingerprint Identification." *UCLA Law Review* 59 (2012): 1252–90.

Rendall, Steve, and Tara Broughel. "Amplifying Officials, Squelching Dissent: FAIR Study Finds Democracy Poorly Served by War Coverage." *Fairness & Accuracy in Reporting*, May 1, 2003.

Renshon, Jonathan. "Assessing Capabilities in International Politics: Biased Overestimation and the Case of the Imaginary 'Missile Gap.'" *Journal of Strategic Studies* 32 (2009): 115–47.

Renshon, Jonathan, and Stanley A. Renshon. "The Enduring Legacy of Alexander L. George: A Symposium." *Political Psychology* 29 (2008): 553–69.

Renshon, Stanley Allen. *The Psychological Assessment of Presidential Candidates*. New York: New York University Press, 1996.

Ricks, Thomas E. *Fiasco: The American Military Adventure in Iraq*. New York: Penguin, 2006.

Risen, Jane, and Thomas Gilovich. "Informal Logical Fallacies." In *Critical Thinking in Psychology*, edited by Robert Sternberg, Henry L. Roediger, and Diane F. Halpern, 110–30. Cambridge: Cambridge University Press, 2007.

Rothkopf, David J. *Running the World: The Inside Story of the National Security Council and the Architects of American Power*. New York: Public Affairs, 2004.

Rutledge, Ian. *Addicted to Oil*. London: I. B. Tauris, 2005.

Samuelson, William, and Richard Zeckhauser. "Status Quo Bias in Decision Making." *Journal of Risk and Uncertainty* 1 (1988): 7–59.

Sandler, Todd, and Daniel G. Arce. "Pure Public Goods versus Commons: Benefit–Cost Duality." *Land Economics* 79 (2003): 355–68.

Sanna, Lawrence J., and Norbert Schwarz. "Integrating Temporal Biases: The Interplay of Focal Thoughts and Accessibility Experiences." *Psychological Science* 15 (2004): 474–81.

Savitsky, Kenneth, and Thomas Gilovich. "The Illusion of Transparency and the Alleviation of Speech Anxiety." *Journal of Experimental Social Psychology* 39 (2003): 618–25.

Schafer, Mark, and Scott Crichlow. *Groupthink versus High-Quality Decision Making in International Relations.* New York: Columbia University Press, 2010.

Scheuer, Michael. *Imperial Hubris: Why the West Is Losing the War on Terror.* Washington, DC: Brassey's, 2004.

———. *Through Our Enemies' Eyes: Osama bin Laden, Radical Islam, and the Future of America.* Washington, DC: Potomac Books, 2006.

Schkade, David, and Daniel Kahneman. "Does Living in California Make People Happy? A Focusing Illusion in Judgments of Life Satisfaction." *Psychological Science* 9 (1998): 340–46.

Schwartz, Barry. *The Paradox of Choice: Why More Is Less.* New York: Ecco, 2003.

Schweitzer, Yoram, and Sari Goldstein Ferber. *Al-Qaeda and the Internationalization of Suicide Terrorism.* Tel Aviv: Jaffee Center for Strategic Studies, Tel Aviv University, 2005.

Schweitzer, Yoram, and Shaul Shay. *The Globalization of Terror: The Challenge of Al-Qaida and the Response of the International Community.* New Brunswick, NJ: Transaction, 2003.

Scowcroft, Brent. "Don't Attack Saddam." *Wall Street Journal*, August 15, 2002.

Sevdalis, Nick, and Nigel Harvey. "Reducing the Impact Bias in Judgments of Post-Decisional Affect: Distraction or Task Interference?" *Judgment and Decision Making* 4 (2009): 287–96.

Shanker, Thom. "New Strategy Vindicates Ex-Army Chief Shinseki." *New York Times*, January 12, 2007.

Shermer, Michael. *The Believing Brain.* New York: Henry Holt, 2011.

Silverman, Barry G. "Modeling and Critiquing the Confirmation Bias in Human Reasoning." *IEEE Transactions on Systems, Man, and Cybernetics* 22 (1992): 972–82.

Silverstein, Brett. "Enemy Images: The Psychology of U.S. Attitudes and Cognitions Regarding the Soviet Union." *American Psychologist* 44 (1989): 903–13.

Singer, Eric, and Valerie Hudson, eds. *Political Psychology and Foreign Policy.* Boulder, CO: Westview Press, 1992.

Sipes, Kristin N., and Robert Mendelsohn. "The Effectiveness of Gasoline Taxation to Manage Air Pollution." *Ecological Economics* 36 (2001): 299–309.

Sissine, Fred. "Energy Independence and Security Act of 2007: A Summary of Major Provisions." Washington, DC: Congressional Research Service, 2007.

Smil, Vaclav. *Energy at the Crossroads.* Cambridge, MA: MIT Press, 2003.

Sperling, Daniel, and James S. Cannon, eds. *Reducing Climate Impacts in the Transportation Sector.* Dordrecht: Springer, 2007.

Speth, James. *Red Sky at Morning: America and the Crisis of the Global Environment.* New Haven, CT: Yale University Press, 2005.

Stanovich, Keith E., and Richard F. West. "Individual Differences in Reasoning: Implications for the Rationality Debate?" *Behavioral and Brain Sciences* 23 (2000): 645–65.

Stein, Janice Gross. "Building Politics into Psychology: The Misperception of Threat." *Political Psychology* 9 (1988): 245–71.

————. "Foreign Policy Decision-Making: Rational, Psychological, and Neurological Models." In *Foreign Policy: Theories, Actors, Cases*, edited by Steve Smith, Amelia Hadfield, and Timothy Dunne, 101–16. Oxford: Oxford University Press, 2008.

Steiner, E. *Consumer Views on Transportation and Energy: Technical Report*, Golden, CO: National Renewable Energy Laboratory, 2003.

Stern, Jessica. *The Ultimate Terrorists*. Cambridge, MA: Harvard University Press, 1999.

Stiglitz, Joseph, and Karen Bilmes. "The Three Trillion Dollar War." *The Times*, February 23, 2008.

Strober, Deborah Hart, and Gerald S. Strober. *The Reagan Presidency: An Oral History of the Era*. Washington, DC: Brassey's, 2003.

Swann, William B., Brett W. Pelham, and Douglas S. Krull. "Agreeable Fancy or Disagreeable Truth? Reconciling Self-Enhancement and Self-Verification." *Journal of Personality and Social Psychology* 57 (1989): 782–91.

Taleb, Nassim Nicholas. *Fooled by Randomness: The Hidden Role of Chance in Life and in the Markets*. New York: Random House, 2005.

————. *The Black Swan: The Impact of the Highly Improbable*. New York: Random House, 2010.

Taliaferro, Jeffrey W. *Balancing Risks: Great Power Intervention in the Periphery*. Ithaca, NY: Cornell University Press, 2004.

Tenet, George J. *Worldwide Threat—Converging Dangers in a Post 9/11 World, Before the Senate Select Committee on Intelligence*, 107th Cong., 2nd sess., February 6, 2002.

————. *At the Center of the Storm: My Years at the CIA*. New York: HarperCollins, 2007.

Tetlock, Philip E. "Accountability and the Perseverance of First Impressions." *Social Psychology Quarterly* 46 (1983): 285–92.

————. *Expert Political Judgment: How Good Is It? How Can We Know?* Princeton, NJ: Princeton University Press, 2006.

Thaler, Richard H., and Cass R. Sunstein. *Nudge: Improving Decisions about Health, Wealth, and Happiness*. New Haven, CT: Yale University Press, 2008.

Thrall, A. Trevor, and Jane K. Cramer, eds. *American Foreign Policy and the Politics of Fear: Threat Inflation since 9/11*. London: Routledge, 2009.

Tower, John G., Edmund S. Muskie, and Brent Scowcroft. *The Tower Commission Report*. New York: Bantam Books, 1987.

Turrentine, Thomas S. "Car Buyers and Fuel Economy?" *Energy Policy* 35 (2007): 1213–23.

Turrentine, Thomas S., Kenneth S. Kurani, and Reid R. Heffner. *Fuel Economy: What Drives Consumer Choice?* Davis: Institute of Transportation Studies, University of California, 2008.

Tversky, Amos, and Daniel Kahneman. "Judgment under Uncertainty: Heuristics and Biases." *Science*, n.s., 185 (1974): 1124–31.

————. "The Framing of Decisions and the Psychology of Choice." *Science*, n.s., 211 (1981): 453–58.

————. "Extensional versus Intuitive Reasoning: The Conjunction Fallacy in Probability Judgment." *Psychological Review* 90 (1983): 293–315.

————. "Advances in Prospect Theory: Cumulative Representation of Uncertainty." *Journal of Risk and Uncertainty* 5 (1992): 297–323.

Vallone, Robert, and Amos Tversky. "The Hot Hand in Basketball: On the Misperception of Random Sequences." *Cognitive Psychology* 17 (1985): 295–314.

Vance, Cyrus. *Hard Choices: Critical Years in America's Foreign Policy.* New York: Simon & Schuster, 1983.

van de Ven, Niels, Thomas Gilovich, and Marcel Zeelenberg. "Delay, Doubt, and Decision: How Delaying a Choice Reduces the Appeal of (Descriptively) Normative Options." *Psychological Science* (2010): 568–73.

Vertzberger, Yaacov. *The World in Their Minds: Information Processing, Cognition, and Perception in Foreign Policy Decisionmaking.* Stanford, CA: Stanford University Press, 1993.

Wallace, Michael D., Peter Suedfeld, and Kimberley Thachuk. "Political Rhetoric of Leaders Under Stress in the Gulf Crisis." *Journal of Conflict Resolution* 37 (1993): 94–107.

Walsh, Lawrence E. *Iran-Contra: The Final Report.* New York: Random House, 1994.

———. *Firewall: The Iran-Contra Conspiracy and Cover-Up.* New York: W.W. Norton, 1997.

Wedeen, Lisa. "Beyond the Crusades: Why Huntington, and Bin Laden, Are Wrong." *Middle East Policy* 10 (2003): 54–61.

Welch, David. *Painful Choices: A Theory of Foreign Policy Change.* Princeton, NJ: Princeton University Press, 2005.

West, Richard F., Russell J. Meserve, and Keith E. Stanovich. "Cognitive Sophistication Does Not Attenuate the Bias Blind Spot." *Journal of Personality and Social Psychology* 103 (2012): 506–19.

Westad, Odd Arne. *The Global Cold War: Third World Interventions and the Making of Our Times.* Cambridge: Cambridge University Press, 2005.

Whitaker, Brian. "Flags in the Dust." *The Guardian,* March 24, 2003.

White, Michael J., Daniel R. Brockett, and Belinda G. Overstreet. "Confirmatory Bias in Evaluating Personality Test Information: Am I Really That Kind of Person?" *Journal of Counseling Psychology* 40 (1993): 120–26.

White, Ralph K. *Fearful Warriors: A Psychological Profile of U.S.-Soviet Relations.* New York: Free Press, 1984.

Whitlock, Craig. "Commandos Free Hostages Being Held in Saudi Arabia." *Washington Post,* May 30, 2004.

Whitson, Jennifer A., and Adam D. Galinksy. "Lacking Control Increases Illusory Pattern Perception." *Science* 322 (2008): 115–17.

Wiktorowicz, Quintan. "The New Global Threat: Transnational Salafis and Jihad." *Middle East Policy* 8 (2001): 18–38.

Wilson, Joseph. *The Politics of Truth: Inside the Lies That Led to War and Betrayed My Wife's CIA Identity.* New York: Carroll & Graf, 2005.

Woodward, Bob. *Bush at War.* New York: Simon & Schuster, 2002.

———. *Plan of Attack.* New York: Simon & Schuster, 2004.

———. *State of Denial.* New York: Simon & Schuster, 2006.

Wright, Lawrence. *The Looming Tower: Al-Qaeda and the Road to 9/11.* New York: Knopf, 2006.

Wright, Robin B. *Sacred Rage: The Wrath of Militant Islam.* New York: Simon & Schuster, 2001.

Yafee, Steven L. "Why Environmental Policy Nightmares Recur." *Conservation Biology* 11 (1997): 328–37.

Yergin, Daniel. *The Prize: The Epic Quest for Oil, Money, and Power.* New York: Simon & Schuster, 1991.

Yetiv, Steve A. *America and the Persian Gulf: The Third Party Dimension in World Politics.* Westport, CT: Praeger, 1995.

————. *The Absence of Grand Strategy: The United States in the Persian Gulf, 1972–2005.* Baltimore: Johns Hopkins University Press, 2008.

————. *Explaining Foreign Policy: U.S. Decision-Making and the Persian Gulf War.* Baltimore: Johns Hopkins University Press, 2011.

————. *The Petroleum Triangle: Oil, Globalization, and Terror.* Ithaca, NY: Cornell University Press, 2011.

Yetiv, Steve A., and Eric S. Fowler. "The Challenges of Decreasing Oil Consumption." *Political Science Quarterly* 126 (2011): 287–313.

Zak, Paul. *The Moral Molecule: The Source of Love and Prosperity.* London: Dutton, 2012.

Zawahiri, Ayman al-. "The Importance of Afghanistan for the Islamist Revolution." In *Anti-American Terrorism and the Middle East,* edited by Barry Rubin and Judith Colp Rubin, 47–49. Oxford: Oxford University Press, 2004.